THE
Shadowhunter's
Codex

BEING a RECORD of
the WAYS and LAWS of the NEPHILIM,
the CHOSEN of the ANGEL RAZIEL

AS COMPILED BY

CASSANDRA CLARE
and JOSHUA LEWIS

Twenty-Seventh English Edition, 1990

First Revision, 2002

Alicante, Idris

Second Revision, 2007,
Clary Fray, Brooklyn, NY, USA
THIRD REVISION, 2007, SIMON LEWIS, BOOK STOLEN FROM CLARY
WHILE SHE TRIES TO STUDY, FUNKYTOWN, USA

WALKER
BOOKS

Fourth Revision, 2007, Jace Wayland
Gives Book Back to Clary and Glares at Simon, USA

First published in Great Britain 2013 by Walker Books Ltd
87 Vauxhall Walk, London SE11 5HJ

2 4 6 8 10 9 7 5 3 1

© 2013 Cassandra Claire LLC
Cover photo-illustration © 2013 Cliff Nielsen

The right of Cassandra Clare and Joshua Lewis to be identified
as authors of this work has been asserted by them in accordance
with the Copyright, Designs and Patents Act 1988

This book has been typeset in Dolly

Printed and bound in Italy

British Library Cataloguing in Publication Data:
a catalogue record for this book is
available from the British Library

ISBN 978-1-4063-5148-4

www.walker.co.uk

CONTENTS

Welcome and Congratulations. You have been chosen to become one of the Nephilim. Soon, if you have not done so already, you will drink from the Mortal Cup, taking into yourself the blood of angels, and you will become one of the "Shadowhunters," named for the founder of our order. Our eternal work is the battle against the forces of darkness that encroach upon our world. We also keep the peace in the Shadow World—the hidden societies of magic and magical creatures wrought by the demons we fight—and keep it hidden from the mundane world. And this now is also *your* charge. You are protector, defender, knight errant in the name of the angels. You will be trained to fight demons, to protect mundanes, to negotiate the complex landscape of the Downworlders—werewolves, vampires, and the like—that you will encounter. Your life will be spent in the pursuit of the angelic against the demonic. And when you die, you will die with glory.

This may appear an intimidating description of the Shadowhunter's life, but we must emphasize the sacredness and the weight of our mission. Joining the Nephilim is not like becoming a mundane policeman, or even a mundane soldier. "Shadowhunter" is not *what you do*; it is *who you are*. Every aspect of your life will change to accommodate the holy assignment you have been chosen for.

This Codex serves to assist you in acclimating to the new world into which you have been thrust. Most Shadowhunters are born into this life, raised and immersed in it constantly from birth, and thus many things about the world that are second nature to them will be new to you. You have been recruited out of your mundane life, and you will quickly encounter much that is confusing and dangerous. This book is designed specifically to reduce your confusion and, ideally, to keep you alive long enough to become a full Shadowhunter in good standing in your local Institute.

It goes without saying that it is against the Law for the Codex to be shared with any persons other than Shadowhunters and mundanes in the process of Ascension (see "Intermarriage," page 187).

WHAT IS A SHADOWHUNTER?

The Nephilim are the appointed warriors on Earth of the Angel Raziel. We are appointed specifically to control and preside over the demonic in our world, both demons and the supernatural creatures born of their presence among us. A thousand years ago Raziel bestowed on us the tools to accomplish this task. These tools are:

—The Mortal Instruments, by which we may know truth, speak with angels, and make more of our own kind

—The country of Idris, in which we may live safely away from both demons and the mundane world

—The Book of Raziel (or "Gray Book"), with which we may make use of the magic of angels to protect and augment ourselves

These were gifts given by Raziel to the first Nephilim, Jonathan Shadowhunter, and so after him we call ourselves Shadowhunters.

Yeah yeah yeah. Get to where I learn kung-fu!

SURE IS CONVENIENT THAT HE WAS NAMED THAT ALREADY. IT MAKES A GOOD NAME FOR THEM.

THE SHADOWHUNTER OATH

There have been many versions of the oath that is spoken by new Nephilim when they drink from the Mortal Cup and join our ranks. The one currently in use was created a little more than a hundred years ago, as part of the reforms that swept through the Shadow World around that time. It replaced an older oath whose language was very martial in tone and that focused mostly on the fact that Shadowhunters are good at killing things. Typically at that time the oath was spoken in one of several holy languages—Latin, Sanskrit, Hebrew, et cetera—and thus was treated more as a formality to execute rather than words to listen to and reflect upon.

The oath follows. You should commit it to memory. At the time you are made a Shadowhunter, you will need to recite it without any prompting. Many new Shadowhunters have complained that this is an unnecessary burden, to which we respond that half-angelic soldiers against the dark forces of the world should not be fazed by the need to memorize a hundred words.

I hereby swear:

I will be Raziel's Sword, extending his arm to strike down evil.
I will be Raziel's Cup, offering my blood to our mission.
I will be Raziel's Mirror; when my enemies behold me, let them see his face in mine.

I hereby promise:

3

I will serve with the angels' courage.
I will serve the angels' justice.
And I will serve with the angels' mercy.

Until such time as I shall die, I will be Nephilim. I pledge myself in Covenant as a Nephilim, and I pledge my life and my family to the Clave of Idris.

It's not like that—there's a zillion laws you're agreeing to follow. It's covered by the "in Covenant."

Would think the oath would be longer?

SHADOWHUNTER NAMES

That coincidence—beggars belief.

A 60 ft tall angel appears to you— apparently does not beggar belief.

Most Ascending mundanes like yourself give up their family name in favor of creating a traditional Shadowhunter name. By tradition most Shadowhunter family names are compound, like "Shadowhunter" itself—in this case, "shadow" + "hunter." Jonathan Shadowhunter's name was, obviously, not actually "Shadowhunter"—such a coincidence would beggar belief. NM, MY COMPLAINT HAS BEEN ANTICIPATED. CODEX 1, ME O.

What Jonathan Shadowhunter was called, before he was made the first Nephilim by Raziel, is lost to history; we do not even know from what country he came. He was given the name Shadowhunter by Raziel (often found written as separate or hyphenated words, as in "Shadow-Hunter," earlier in history) as a symbol of his transformation. According to many tellings of the story, Raziel told Jonathan, "I grant you the light and fire of angels, to illuminate your way in dark, for you and your companions will be Hunters of the Shadows." LIKE MASTERS OF THE UNIVERSE™ Not much like them no

There is a kind of poetry in the selection of a Shadowhunter family name; combining just any two things into a name is not enough. Your name should try to reflect something about who you are, or where you're from, or what you hope to be. In order to stimulate ideas of your own, we here supply a list of appropriate English words that can be combined to make names. Simply select

WAIT TILL YOU MEET JONATHAN UNIVERSEMASTER.

4

two of them and put them next to each other. Usually they will sound better in one order than in the other order.

NOTE: USE YOUR JUDGMENT. Your name must be approved by those evaluating your petition for Ascension. Do not try to name yourself Dragonrider or Firedance or Elfstar. Nephilim are meant to be inconspicuous. Obviously things such as Hammerfist or Bloodsteel should also be avoided.

ALDER	GOLD	SCAR
APPLE	GRAY	SHADE
ASH	GREEN	SHADOW
ASPEN	HALLOW	SILVER
BAY	HAWK	STAIR
BEAR	HEAD	STARK
BLACK	HEART	STORM
BLOOD	HERON	THRUSH
BLUE	HOOD	TOWER
BOW	HUNTER	TREE
BRANDY	KEY	WAIN
BROWN	LAND	WALKER
BULL	LIGHT	WATER
CAR	MAPLE	WAY
CART	MARK	WEATHER
CHERRY	MERRY	WELL
CHILD	NIGHT	WHEEL
COCK	OWL	WHITE
CROSS	PEN	WINE
DOVE	PINE	WOLF
EARTH	RAVEN	WOOD
FAIR	RED	WRIGHT
FISH	ROSE	YOUNG
FOX	SCALE	

What is your Shadowhunter name?

Fairchild.

Can't believe you actually wrote that in.

Definitely either STORMWALKER

or NIGHTRAVEN—what do you think?

BLOODSUCKER fits.

Not cool bro

THE SHADOWHUNTER'S GLOSSARY

Shouldn't that be "glossarie"?

The world you are entering is a secret one. It is kept hidden from the vast majority of the mundane world, who do not know even that our kind exist, much less the many varieties of ~~monster~~

∧ HANDSOME INDIVIDUAL

among whom we are responsible for keeping peace. Naturally, the denizens of that world may make common reference to places and things with which you are not yet familiar. We thus provide this handy short guide to some of the more common terms, which will be explored in more depth in later chapters as warranted.

Well, thank goodness.

PEOPLE AND PLACES

We are called *Nephilim* or *Shadowhunters*. We are the children of men and *angels*; the Angel *Raziel* gave us our power.

Our primary mission is to eliminate *demons*, who come in a large

Hey.

I don't know you. I can't guess who you might be. But I'm done with this Codex now, and I think it's time I pass it on.

Okay, I've written all over it. And . . . drawn all over it. But I think it's better than a fresh clean Codex, because I've corrected some stuff and added some things. I think it's more true, has less of the political stuff the Clave puts in to make themselves look good.

So this is yours now. Whoever you are. If you need to find this, you'll find it.

Anyway, welcome. This is the Codex. I always thought it was like this great tome of wisdom, but it's more like an army field manual—how you teach someone to be a Shadowhunter when you're already being chased by demons. So I'm not the usual reader. Luckily, Jace has added some notes too. He's taking my training a little too seriously, by the way. I think it's because everyone already thinks we're just pretending to train and actually making out. So, he's Jace, he has to prove them wrong. Hence real serious training. Which is why I am writing this with an icepack on my hip, by the way.

Simon has appeared to announce that the Codex reminds him of a Dungeons & Dragons manual. "Like, you know, it tells you the rules. Vampires are weak to . . . fire! They bite you for 2d10 damage with their vicious fangs!" Now he is making a bitey face at me. He kind of looks like a hamster. Seriously, I love Simon, but he is like the worst vampire ever.

Simon, you don't have to make pretend fangs with your fingers. You have actual fangs.

Why Do People Become Shadowhunters, by Magnus Bane

This Codex thing is very silly. Downworlders talk about the Codex like it is some great secret full of esoteric knowledge, but really it's a Boy Scout manual.

One thing that it mysteriously doesn't address is *why* people become Shadowhunters. And you should know that people become Shadowhunters for many stupid reasons.

So here is an addition to your copy.

Greetings, young aspiring Shadowhunter-to-be—or possibly already technically a Shadowhunter. I can't remember whether you drink from the Cup first or get the book first. Regardless, congratulations. You have just been recruited by the Monster Police. You may be wondering, why? *Why of all the mundanes out there was I selected and invited to this exclusive club made up largely, at least from a historical perspective, of murderous psychopaths?*

Possible Reasons Why:
1. You possess a stout heart, strong will, and able body.
2. You possess a stout body, able will, and strong heart.
3. Local Shadowhunters are ironically punishing you by making you join them.
4. You were recruited by a local Institute to join the Nephilim as an ironic punishment for your mistreatment of Downworlders.
5. Your home, village, or nation is under siege by demons.
6. Your home, village, or nation is under siege by rogue Downworlders.
7. You were in the wrong place at the wrong time.

8. You know too much, and should be recruited because the secrecy of the Shadow World has already been compromised for you.

9. You know too little; it would be helpful to the Shadowhunters if you knew more.

10. You know exactly the right amount, making you a natural recruit.

11. You possess a natural resistance to glamour magic and must be recruited to keep you quiet and provide you with some basic protection.

12. You have a compound last name already and convinced someone important that yours *is* a Shadowhunter family and the Shadowhunteriness has just been weakened by generations of poor breeding.

13. You had a torrid affair with a member of the Nephilim Council, and now he's trying to cover his tracks.

14. Shadowhunters are concerned they are no longer haughty and condescending enough—have sought you out to add a much needed boost of haughty condescension.

15. You have been bitten by a radioactive Shadowhunter, giving you the proportional strength and speed of a Shadowhunter.

16. Large bearded man on flying motorcycle appeared to take you away to Shadowhunter school. (Note: Presence of flying motorcycle suggests bearded man may be a vampire.)

17. Your mom has been in hiding from your evil dad, and you found out you're a Shadowhunter only a few weeks ago.

That's right. Seventeen reasons. Because that's how many I thought of. Now run off, little Shadowhunter, and learn to murder things. And be nice to Downworlders.

variety of species and forms. We also seek to keep the peace among several populations of demihumans, known collectively as *Downworlders*. These groups are *werewolves, vampires, faeries*, and *warlocks*. We preside over a treaty known as the *Accords* that ordains how we and all of these groups may interact, as well as each group's rights, responsibilities, and restrictions. The Accords are revised and signed every fifteen years by representatives of the Nephilim and all Downworlder groups.

We have our own secret country, which is hidden in Central Europe and is known as *Idris*. Its capital city—indeed, its only city—is named *Alicante*, and that is where the Council resides, and where Clave meetings are held (see below).

Most Shadowhunters spend their younger years as warriors. The exceptions are the members of our two monastic orders, the *Silent Brothers* and the *Iron Sisters*. The Brothers serve as our keepers of lore and knowledge: They are our librarians, our researchers, our medics. They reside in the *Silent City*, a place deep underground, many of whose levels are kept secret even from normal Shadowhunters. The Sisters design and forge our weapons; they are the keepers of *adamas*, the holy metal given by Raziel for our use. They reside in the *Adamant Citadel*, which is even more hidden than the Silent City; except for a single receiving chamber, it can be entered only by Iron Sisters. *Obsessed with secrecy? A little?*

CLAVE, COUNCIL, CONSUL, COVENANT

The *Clave* is the collective name for the political body made up of all active Nephilim. All Shadowhunters that recognize the authority of Idris—and this should be all of them in the world who remain Shadowhunters—make up the Clave. When Shadowhunters reach adulthood at the age of eighteen, they declare their allegiance to the Clave and become full Clave members, with rights to contribute to any Clave issue under discussion. The Clave keeps and interprets the Law, and makes decisions about the guidance of the Nephilim through history as it unfolds. *What if you don't declare allegiance? That's called "leaving the Shadowhunters." It'll be covered later.*

Smaller, more regional groups of Shadowhunters, for instance the Shadowhunters of a specific country or sometimes of a particularly large city, are collected in what are called Enclaves in most of the world, and Conclaves in the Americas and Australia. These regional groups coordinate their own local decision making and organizational structures as they see fit, although the Clave as a whole is responsible for placing Shadowhunters in charge of specific Institutes. The Clave may intercede in cases where an Enclave or Conclave is organized in some way that is against the spirit of the Nephilim as a whole (for instance, in cases where some individual Shadowhunter has tried to seize dictatorial power over nearby Downworlders, as with the infamous cult of personality and human sacrifice declared by Hezekiah Short in the Mayan ruins of southeastern Mexico in the 1930s).

The term "Clave" comes from the Latin *clavis*, meaning "key," and its use in such terms as "Enclave" and "Conclave" refers abstractly to the idea of an assembly "under lock and key"—that is, meeting in secret. The Clave is, so to speak, the great secret of the Nephilim; with the key of the Mortal Cup, one earns entrance to its chambers.

The *Council* is the governing body of the Clave. Once, there were few enough Shadowhunters in the world that in matters of importance the entire Clave could be canvassed for their opinion, but it has been many hundreds of years since this was the case. The Council does, however, in representing the larger Clave, retain the power to recall any Shadowhunter to Idris at any time. Today local Enclaves choose representatives to sit on the Council, which deals with matters of immediate import that are not large enough for the entire Clave to become involved in. Enclaves may decide for themselves how to appoint their Council representatives. Most times this is accomplished with a simple vote or by the Conclave head appointing a chosen delegate; sometimes the Conclave head sits on the Council herself. Some regions have more colorful means of appointing their representative. For instance, in eighteenth-century France under the Sun King, the Council delegate was appointed by means of a dance competition. The Saint Petersburg Enclave to this day holds a massive annual chess tournament; the competitor who loses the most matches is named the Council delegate.

The *Consul* is the highest appointed official in the Clave. He is something like a prime minister rather than like a king or president; he wields little executive power but rather serves to preside over the Council, to officially tally its votes, and to help interpret the Law for the Clave. He also serves as an adviser to the Inquisitor, and is intended to be a consulting mentor for the heads of Institutes. His only real source of direct power is his authority to call the Council to session and to adjudicate disputes between Shadowhunters. The Nephilim do not have such uncivilized mundane notions as political parties; the Consul is voted into office by the Council and, like most prime ministers, can be put out of office by a vote of no confidence.

Tying all of these entities together is the *Covenant*, another name for Nephilim Law. It provides the rules of conduct for Shadowhunters and Downworlders; it is by the right of Covenant that the Nephilim enforce their Law in Downworld. (There have been times and places where that rule of Law has been held in place by force rather than by Covenant, but we happily live in more enlightened times today.) The Covenant protects the rights of Shadowhunters to enforce civilized relations among the Clave, Downworld, and the mundane world, and also protects the rights of Downworlders so that they may not be maltreated by Shadowhunters.

It is the Covenant also that guarantees that the Shadow World remains shadowed from the mundane world. Nephilim are sworn by Covenant never to reveal the truth of the world to a mundane, unless such a revelation cannot in any way be avoided. All Downworlders who have signed the Accords agree to the same. Demons are the great unpredictable force in keeping the Shadow World secret, but so far demons have decided that secrecy is best for them as well.

This description makes the Covenant sound simple, but its fine print is more or less the entire legal system of the Shadowhunters, specifying not only the criminal code that the Nephilim and various Downworlder communities have agreed to abide by, but also how that criminal code may be prosecuted, how trials may be run, and so on. This means both Shadowhunters and Downworlders may refer to the Covenant to claim some specific right. For instance, Shadowhunters may swear upon the Covenant to keep information confidential that has been shared with them in an investigation.

The Covenant long precedes the Accords; the Accords can be seen as a kind of Bill of Rights, amendments to the Covenant that are agreed to be taken as the law of the land by all of the Shadow World.

DISCUSSION QUESTIONS AND THINGS TO TRY

1. What do you notice about the kinds of words that are used to make up Shadowhunter names? What do they have in common? What might this say about the Shadowhunters' identity and what family names are supposed to represent?

SIMON NIGHTRAVEN NEEDS NO DISCUSSION QUESTIONS.

It's not your book, Simon.　　YOU DON'T NEED DISCUSSION QUESTIONS EITHER,
CLARY HORSEPHONE.

2. Do you know who your local Council member is? Do you know who runs your local Institutes? Find out!

Yes. Yes. Okay. **WHO**

That's not what it says!
SEE ME

3. Try: Introducing yourself to a Silent Brother! Their appearance may be intimidating, but you will find them to be friendly and patient. (Note: Do not try to introduce yourself to an Iron Sister at this time.)

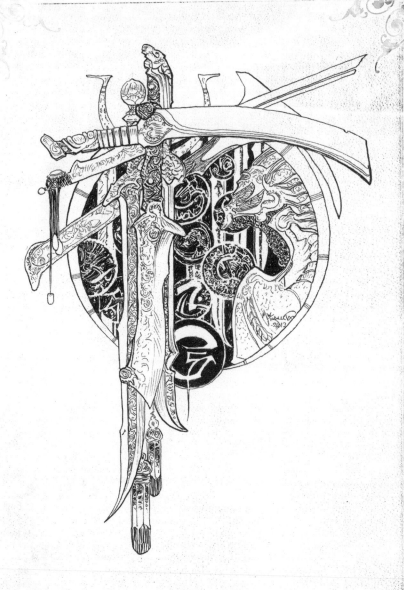

CHAPTER ONE

TREASURY

ARMS

CHOOSING A WEAPON

Shadowhunters do not use firearms, and typically we fight in close quarters. We also usually fight in short, improvised confrontations rather than in planned battles. As such, the basic armaments of the Shadowhunters are those hand-to-hand weapons that humans have used for thousands of years. Each of these come in endless variations, and you will need to tune your training to the specifics of your locale. Here we endeavor to lay out the categories of weapons and briefly discuss their pros and cons.

You should plan to quickly achieve a basic competence in each of these categories. Remember that demons are infinite in type and variety; a Shadowhunter never knows when she might face a foe against whom her preferred weapons are totally useless. You should, however, also give thought to what kind of weapon you might choose to specialize in. Some feel called to the longsword, while others will have a natural gift with a bow and arrow. Finding the intersection of your interest and your talent is a major goal of your early training.

 Any decently stocked Institute should have on hand a selection of all of the weapons mentioned here, in addition to other basic useful combat tools such as: binding wire of silver, gold, and/or electrum; wooden stakes in oak and

ash; amulets of protection; assorted holy symbols for major world religions; and basic magic implements (chalk, iron filings, small vial of animal blood, etc.). A truly well-stocked large Institute might add to that list such specialty items as lead swords, holy trumpets, bone staves, etc., depending on location.

Did you know?

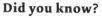

Shadowhunter weapons are Marked with runes. While only seraph blades can cause permanent harm to demons, angelic Marks on other weapons will at least slow a demon's recovery from a wound. Without these Marks, demons easily shrug off the effects of our physical weapons.

SWORDS

Swords are long hilted blades used to wound both by piercing and by slashing. Variants range from light and flexible blades wielded in one hand, such as the rapier, to heavy blades such as the Scottish claymore that require two hands to wield and whose blades may well be taller than a person. And more or less all possible stages in between are represented. Generally Shadowhunters have a preference for speed and agility in fighting, and so most who prefer swords specialize in one of the smaller one-handed versions. There are, of course, exceptions. Note that if you have never wielded a sword before, you may be surprised by how quickly your arm will grow tired, even when using a light blade. If you have never used a sword before, you can get an early start on training by practicing simply holding a sword out in front of your body, parallel to the ground, for a length of time. You will be ready to start actual combat training when you can keep the sword steady for thirty minutes.

KNIVES AND DAGGERS

These smaller blades are less tiring to hold, and frequently two are wielded at the same time. The trade-off is, of course, that they have a shorter reach than a sword, requiring you to be closer to your foe. They are also far easier to conceal than a sword. Seraph blades are typically wielded using techniques associated with dagger fighting, so you will want to grow proficient with these weapons no matter what. *Thank you, Codex, because I didn't know what a knife was.*

You may also learn to throw knives and daggers, but it's a very difficult skill to pick up, and daggers are usually more difficult and expensive to create than arrows, considering that you may lose them after a single use. Still, many Shadowhunters favor the throwing skill for its showy nature. *Haha Jace throws knives because of his showy nature.*

We were all 14 once. You'd have learned it too if you could have.

MACES, AXES, HAMMERS, ETC. *Touché, whatever your last name is.*

Those who do not seek subtlety in their combat may wish to consider specializing in a weapon in these categories, whereby the enemy is simply bludgeoned with a heavy block of metal, possibly sharpened. You will come across few creatures that cannot be successfully defeated by the application of sufficient blunt trauma. The main advantage of these weapons is that, while one can learn finesse in wielding them, they tend to be effective even when that finesse is lacking. All the wielder requires is brute strength and room to swing. *Oh please please please Clary. Tiny girl with a gigantic hammer! So anime!*

The main disadvantages of these weapons are that, for one, they can be difficult to conceal, and for another, they depend on the enemy's skin being less strong than the material of the weapon, which is usually true of Downworlders but may often be untrue of demons.

Flails and morning-stars, in which the aforementioned heavy chunk of metal is attached to the handle by a chain and thus can

In real life tiny girl with gigantic hammer has gigantic forearms.

be swung around to build up more momentum, add more force to your blows in exchange for a higher risk of accidentally walloping yourself or the person standing next to you.

POLEARMS, PIKES, SPEARS, LANCES

There are almost as many variations on these as there have been human armies in history, but they all have the same basic structure: a sharp blade at the end of a long sturdy stick. Traditionally these have been used in mundane warfare to give a fighter a longer reach than normal—which can be useful when fighting a foe on horseback (or giant lizard-back, in the case of some demons), a demon covered in tentacles, a demon with obscenely long arms, and so on. Today, however, fighting from horseback is obsolescent, and the annoyance of carrying a sharp six-foot-long pole around is rarely worth the trouble. You are most likely to see these carried by Shadowhunter guards as ceremonial weapons; you are also likely to find that these guards have other weapons on their person that they would wield instead in case of action.

BOWS AND CROSSBOWS

These are the definitive Shadowhunter weapons for long-range fighting. They are lightweight and easy to carry, and you can bring a large number of arrows with you with little trouble. Often Shadowhunters will carry arrows with several different arrowhead materials, useful for fighting different kinds of creatures. (We recommended color-coding the feathers for ease in identification.)

Like sword fighting, archery is a complex and difficult skill, and you will need to train diligently to be able to use it in a real-life scenario. Shadowhunters almost never fire arrows from an entrenched stable position, like someone defending a castle from a siege. Expect to have to arm, aim, and fire your bow while in the middle of total chaos. Do not expect your archery instructor to let you take a bow with you into combat until you have demonstrated some serious skill.

IMPROVISED WEAPONS

The Nephilim are trained in the use of weapons, and our weapons are a vital part of our combat methods. It is important to always remember, however, that a Shadowhunter without fighting weapons is not helpless. The fight against demons is a desperate one, and weapons can be improvised from the environment—a tree branch, an andiron, a handful of pebbles thrown in the face of a foe. Then too the Shadowhunter should always remember that her own body is a weapon. She has been trained to be faster and stronger than mundanes, and in the panic of battle should remember her strength and make use of it. A weapon does not win a battle; the Nephilim wielding the weapon does.

EXOTIC WEAPONS

There are, of course, as many nonstandard and exotic weapons as there are human cultures, and you may find that your local Nephilim have some combat specialties outside the common weapon types. These may include whips, sword canes, obscure weapons of martial arts traditions, household objects modified to double as blades, and so on. These rarer "specialty" weapons are not forbidden or discouraged from use. Indeed, a Shadowhunter is likely to be more effective with a weapon toward which they feel an affinity than with one forced into their hand by the dictates of training protocols.

Two specific exotic weapons are worthy of note here, one angelic, one demonic.

The *aegis* is a dagger that has been seethed and tempered in angel blood. They are incredibly rare, as one

19

would imagine, since angel blood is not easily come by. There are only a small number of these in the hands of the Shadowhunters, and they are kept by the Iron Sisters and are not permitted to reside in an Institute. They are available for requisition in the armory, but the requestor should be prepared with a very good reason for the request. The Iron Sisters are not usually pleased to give them out.

The *athame* is a ceremonial, double-edged dagger, usually with a black handle and carved with demonic runes. It is used in demon-summoning rituals to draw blood or carve lines of magical force and is only for ritual use. The weapon loses its power if used in combat. It is one of the four elemental tools of the neo-pagan mundane religion Wicca; as such there are many false *athame* floating around. Warlocks can of course tell the difference on sight, but mundanes cannot. This can sometimes lead a mundane to accidentally possess a genuine *athame*, which is a great danger.

SERAPH BLADES

There is a legend told of the first seraph blade, which may or may not be true. The legend dates to the earliest days of the Iron Sisters, when they were few in number and the Adamant Citadel was merely a single *adamas* forge and a set of protective wards. In those days the paths from the mundane world to the volcanic plains of the Citadel were not as hidden and guarded as they are now, and it is said that a demon, a Dragon—for in those days Dragon demons were not almost extinct—found its way to the location of the Citadel. There was only a single Sister there working at the forge, and she was caught unawares and unarmed, having placed her faith in the impossibility of the Sisters' forge being found by the enemy.

Laughing and threatening, the Dragon stepped through lava beds as though skipping across shallow streams. In terror, the

Sister cast about her for a weapon, but all she had to hand were irregular jags of *adamas*, recently extracted from ore and waiting to be worked. She seized one and held it between her and the approaching Dragon like a pikeman preparing to receive a charge. Her hand trembled; she was afraid not for her own life but for the continued existence of the Iron Sisters: If the demons could travel here, surely they would overrun the Citadel soon enough.

Panic-stricken, she called out prayers to the forces of good. As the Dragon was upon her, she loudly abjured it in the name of Michael, the slayer of Sammael, general of the armies of Heaven. Promptly the *adamas* jag lit up, blue and brilliant with heavenly fire. The Sister's hand burned where she clutched it, but with all her strength she thrust her makeshift lance and pierced the Dragon in the soft flesh under his jaw. She expected it to wound the Dragon and nothing more—but perhaps it would buy her enough time to flee.

Instead the *adamas* spear bored through the neck of the Dragon as if through paper, and around the spear burst flames of seraphic fire. The Dragon screamed and burned, and as the Sister watched, the demon staggered away from her, damaged in a way she had never seen a demon damaged before. Across the lava moat surrounding the Adamant Forge, the Dragon was overcome, fell to the ground, and burned for an hour.

The Sister fell to her knees in exhaustion and watched the Dragon's carcass slowly fade from the world. She could then have rested—no one would have blamed her—but she was an Iron Sister, and by the time her fellow Sisters found her a few hours later, she had deduced the nature of the power she had uncovered and had drawn up on vellum the first blueprints for the seraph blade.

Iron Sisters: surprisingly badass.

Today seraph blades, or angel blades, are the fundamental weapon in Shadowhunter combat. They are as clear as glass,

21

usually double-edged, and normally about two feet in length. Being *adamas*, they are incredibly finely honed and are capable of holding their edge indefinitely. They are thus potent weapons against any foe. Their true power, however, is revealed when they are named—when a Shadowhunter holds them and invokes the name of an angel. The spirit of that angel is said to then inhabit the blade for a time, and the weapon will glow brightly with heavenly fire, like the flaming sword of the angel who guards the Garden of Eden.

This heavenly fire is very potent against demons. Most demons can heal themselves from mundane injuries in our world fairly quickly, just as werewolves and vampires can. We Mark our mundane weapons (see sections below) to make them more potent, but even so, the best we can do with them is damage demons enough that they must retreat to lick their wounds, as it were. Only the seraph blade can *permanently* damage a demon, so that it must withdraw for more significant and lengthy healing or must return to the Void to repair itself.

After a time the power of an activated seraph blade will be exhausted, and it will need to be refreshed by the Iron Sisters in order to be used again. Depleted seraph blades can be brought to the weapons room of your local Institute for regular recycling.

Iron Sisters also fuckers at recycling!

Note that the seraph blade is a viable but drastically overpowered weapon in a fight against a mundane. Downworlders are harmed by them in much the same manner as demons, but mundane flesh pierced by a seraph blade will burst into flame and may consume the mundane entirely. THE CLAVE HAS OFFICIALLY DEEMED THIS "AWESOME"

Shadowhunters will not be so burned by seraph blades, given our angelic blood, but even so, activated blades can severely burn the wielder's hands, and you should not touch a seraph blade until you have been Marked with the rune of Angelic Power. (Typically this is placed either at the base of the throat or on the inside of each wrist.) A Shadowhunter who has been stabbed by a seraph blade will *not* burst into flames, but it should be remembered that seraph blades are still blades and can kill a Shadowhunter by more terrestrial means, like any other sword or dagger.

By the way, most Shadowhunters think we have to name seraph blades just because Jonathan Shadowhunter thought it was important to make everyone memorize a lot of angel names.

That guy was hard-core.

MATERIALS

It does mean you rule at Angel Trivial Pursuit.

Also Angel Scrabble.

You'll find weapons made of all kinds of materials in your local Institute, chosen for their magical properties.

ADAMAS

Adamas is the heavenly metal granted to the Shadowhunters for our use by the Angel Raziel. The metal is silver-white and translucent, and glows slightly (although this glow may not be visible in broad daylight). It generally feels smooth to the touch, like glass but notably warmer and heavier. It is the hardest substance the Nephilim know of, and cannot be worked by mundane means. The Iron Sisters use seraphic Marks unknown to non-Sisters to shape the metal; to craft weapons and steles from it, the Sisters use forges that take their fire from the heart of a volcano.

IRON

This element is toxic to faeries. You will often encounter the term "cold iron" in reference to the fey; this is just regular iron. The term "cold iron" refers to the fact that it is cold to the touch, which was at one time believed to be associated with its magical properties. Iron takes enchantment and blessing very well. It's generally believed that it is the large quantity of iron in human blood that causes its affinity for enchantment. It is especially worth mentioning that meteoric iron, the nickel-iron alloy that makes up many meteors, is a particularly good conductor of magical energy.

STEEL

This type of iron alloy is usually *not* toxic to faeries. It is the purity of iron that grants its power over the fey. Steel does, however, hold a sharpened edge very well, and thus the Shadowhunter will normally spend a large amount of time training with steel weaponry to learn how to put one of those sharpened edges through a demon.

SILVER

Silver is a metal with which all Nephilim are intimately familiar. Using a weapon made of silver is one of the only ways to permanently injure a werewolf, who will heal from a wound made by any other material. The element is toxic to vampires and causes them to experience pain, headaches, nausea, and so on, though it will not kill them. Silver is a potent conductor of magical energies, behind only gold and *adamas*, and as a result the fey also use a large amount of it in both their arms and armor, and also in their decorative arts. Shadowhunters have the unenviable task of learning to wield both steel and silver weapons, which differ noticeably in weight, and the Shadowhunter must in fact learn to switch between them quickly.

GOLD

This metal is poisonous to demons. It is also an excellent conductor of magical energies, although it is rarely used to make weapons or tools, since in its pure form it is one of the most soft and pliant metals. Interestingly, it has both strongly positive and strongly negative associations in religious ritual. On the one hand its rarity, resistance to corrosion, and beauty has caused it to be used to symbolize high esteem, power, and the light of Heaven. On the other hand its expense and rarity has made it a symbol of greed and of the profanity of material wealth, as opposed to the sacredness of spiritual wealth. Thus, one will find gold used in sacred and powerful religious decorations and also in some of the darkest of demonic rituals.

ELECTRUM
Electrum is an alloy of gold and silver that can be found naturally in the earth. It has been known and used since the time of the pharaohs of ancient Egypt. Its lack of purity means that it is rarely used in specific rituals, but it is considered a good conductor of magic. It combines the mystical abilities of both silver and gold, in lesser strength than either pure metal but at significantly less expense than pure gold and without some of the disadvantages.

COPPER
This element is used mostly as an intensifier for other materials. It is thought to help bring the abilities of other metals into better alignment with the wielder, and thus is often used decoratively, or to form hilts or handles of silver weapons, for instance.

DEMON-METAL
Demon-metal is a noble metal (that is, one resistant to corrosion) that is believed to originate in the Void, and cannot be found naturally in our universe. It is black in appearance but is believed to be transparent and glowing with black demonic power. It is something like the demonic equivalent of *adamas* in that it creates wounds that cannot be easily healed by seraphic Marks and require much more involved medical attention. You will find it

sometimes used to forge weapons or armor wielded or worn by demons themselves. It is incredibly rare to find it in the hands of Downworlders or humans.

ROWAN

The European rowan tree has long been known to have magically protective properties. It has been used in Europe to ward off malevolent spirits and enchantments for thousands of years. These properties, along with the tree's density and strength, have made it a common choice for the staves of druids and other priests, and it is commonly used in the construction of Institutes and for arrows wielded by Nephilim.

ASH

The wood of Yggdrasil, the world-tree of Norse mythology, is believed to be the source of the so-called Mead of Poetry, the mythological beverage that would magically transform the drinker into a scholar. It has properties similar to that of rowan but is notably easier to work. It is also often used in a similar way to iron—it is believed to have a similar affinity with humans. (Norse mythology also cites it as the wood from which the first human was created.)

OAK

The oak tree is often considered the "most mundane" of woods, and from this very fact it draws its power. It has great strength and hardness and is therefore frequently the material of choice for wooden weapons. Stakes for vampire slaying, for instance, are traditionally crafted out of oak, which is believed to help guide the wielder's hand to the source of demonic magic, in order to eliminate it. *Jace is considered the most awesome material to make a Shadowhunter out of.*

26

I AM BOTH GROSSED OUT AND CONFUSED.

HOLY WATER *Batman!*

You probably already know of holy water. In fact the use of
water as a weapon against evil is well-explored in myths and
legends. Water is the substance that, more than any other,
defines and sustains life in our world. It can be made, with
the application of ritual, to take into itself something of
the angelic, to become not merely the water of life but
holy water. Holy water has proved to be a useful weapon
against demonic powers: It is severely toxic to demons and
also to vampires. It can be used to flush out the beginnings
of vampire infection, to save someone who has ingested
vampire blood. (See the Bestiaire Part II, Chapter 4, for more
details.) Faeries, on the other hand, can stand its presence
and its touch but will be made severely weakened and ill if
they can be fooled into drinking it. (Interestingly, werewolves
are not affected by holy water at all, just as they are not at all
negatively affected by other mundane religious objects.)

That actually is interesting! Ask Luke about.

Many mundane religions include this notion of
seraphically aligned water, and it is from the mundanes' holy
men and women that the Nephilim acquire the majority of
our holy water. As part of our relationships with mundane
religions, we maintain connections with monastic orders
across the globe. One of these orders' responsibilities is to
bless water and other objects for the Nephilim. The orders
connected to the Nephilim tend to be among the more
secretive monastic orders, often those sworn to silence, and
the relationships are often kept up by Silent Brothers and
Iron Sisters.

How we collect, store, and distribute all this holy water to the
Institutes and to Idris is a fascinating hydrodynamic engineering
problem that will not be gone into in this text. Those who are

27

interested in more depth are encouraged to visit the Silent City, where the research Brothers there will be more than happy to supply you with the multivolume handwritten tomes they have created specifying the processes, for perusal at your leisure.

No need to be sarcastic, Codex.
I think that's sincere, actually.
Wow.

—— ARMOR AND OTHER TOOLS ——

Black for hunting through the night
For death and mourning the color's white
Gold for a bride in her wedding gown
And red to call enchantment down.
White silk when our bodies burn,
Blue banners when the lost return.
Flame for the birth of a Nephilim,

And to wash away our sins.
Gray for knowledge best untold,
Bone for those who don't grow old.
Saffron lights the victory march,
Green will mend our broken hearts.
Silver for the demon towers,
And bronze to summon wicked powers.

—Old Nephilim children's rhyme

SHADOWHUNTER GEAR

One's first set of Shadowhunter gear is, for most Shadowhunters, an important moment in their training—the time when they begin to first *look* like other Shadowhunters. When you wear gear, you become part of a tradition joining Shadowhunters across hundreds of years; our gear has remained basically unchanged since modern textile methods came into being.

Battle gear is crafted of a well-processed black leather, created by the Iron Sisters in their Citadel, stronger than any mundane leather and capable of protecting the skin from most demon venoms while still allowing for swift and free movement. Nephilim on regular patrols or similar excursions may choose to wear only the basic gear, but those preparing for battle will often add bracers and greaves, traditionally of electrum (see "Materials" page 23).

Both the gear and accessories such as bracers are typically Marked, both with runes of protection and strength and with more decorative symbols. These might include family crests, Marks commemorating battles, names of angels invoked as protectors, and so on.

The standard Shadowhunter gear involves, for both men and women, simple flat-soled shoes and sturdy, closely fit trousers. For most of Nephilim history gear differed between men and women—men would wear with the above a closely fit waist-length shirt and sometimes a jacket, whereas women would wear a long belted knee-length tunic. This tunic was always a less practical choice, and was worn historically to maintain the standards of modesty and decorum that were required of women as they moved through mundane society. In the past fifty years or so, the use of this tunic has faded in favor of more unified, unisex gear worn by male and female Shadowhunters alike.

THE PROBLEMS OF TRADITIONAL ARMOR

Many new Shadowhunters through the years have arrived at their first day of training proudly clad in their family's ancestral plate armor, as if they were going off to fight the Hundred Years' War. (Obviously this problem was at its worst during the actual Hundred Years' War.) In truth this kind of heavy armor is not very useful to Nephilim; standard fighting gear is preferred, and the specifics of the gear are less important than one's weaponry. The mundane world went through a complicated "arms race" through the Middle Ages regarding armor. Both weapons and armor gradually improved in effectiveness, with new weapons designed to pierce armor, and then new armor designed to withstand those weapons. Armor reached its apex with a somewhat ridiculous full suit of steel intended to stop a blade or an arrow, and became rapidly irrelevant with the advent of artillery and firearms in mundane warfare.

Shadowhunters never participated in this silly exercise. First, Shadowhunters have always, by necessity, prioritized such attributes as freedom of movement, detailed assessment of the environment, and swiftness over raw strength of material, and as a result were rarely tempted by heavier, bulkier armor. Second, the fact is that mundane armor is designed to protect the wearer from the attacks of other mundanes. We, on the other hand, frequently face foes who wield magic, and who might on any given day attack us with fire, with excoriating acid, with bolts of demonic lightning, with venoms and poisons of all kinds. We know of no material—including *adamas*—that can keep a Shadowhunter safe from all of the devices at the disposal of our demon foes. We therefore have always had to learn to avoid harm by our wits and reflexes, since no amount of steel covering our bodies would truly keep us safe.

THE EVERYDAY CARRY

Shadowhunters do not typically travel heavily loaded with equipment. What they take with them on patrols or investigations must not slow them down very much, or compromise their agility. Thus they typically prefer small tools, lightweight and easily kept in a pocket. Most Shadowhunters will find a set of tools that they will take with them everywhere; it is worth some time considering what tools you find useful to keep on hand. Some common tools are here suggested, and described in detail where necessary.

TYPICAL SHADOWHUNTER EQUIPMENT
—Gear
—Primary weapon
—Two seraph blades

sling? like with a rock? really?

—Ranged weapon (e.g., crossbow, sling) (Optional)

—Stele *You're kidding. Lame. Okay. Custom lesson from Jace here. Yes, take all that stuff.*

—Witchlight *Actually, carry two witchlights. Some other stuff that I always carry with me on patrol: chalk. A multi-tool with screwdrivers and two knives and a corkscrew and*

—Sensor *all that. A sturdy watch. A strong folding utility knife. A butane lighter. A phone.*

If you are also carrying a backpack, I recommend throwing in nylon rope, a small crowbar, binoculars,

THE SENSOR *a basic first aid kit, a spare stele, two extra seraph blades. Oh, and rubber gloves.*

The Sensor is a common Shadowhunter device for detecting demonic activity. Sensors have varied in design over the years, but today the Sensor is usually a small handheld oblong made of a black metal. It bears some resemblance to a modern cellular phone or other handheld mundane communication device, but where that mundane device would have control buttons and switches labeled in a mundane language, the Sensor is labeled in Marks whose meaning must be learned. The original Sensor was invented in the late 1880s by Henry Branwell and for a time revolutionized the pursuit and capture of demons. *It's a tricorder.* **What? What is a** *tricorder? Three . . . cords?*

Every so often you'll be very glad you have them.

Unfortunately, the Sensor is somewhat limited in what it is able to sense. It functions as a frequency detector, tuning in to the vibrations that demons create as they pass through the magical ether. These vibrations vary by demon species and change in intensity based on the intensity of demon activity (number of demons, demonic magic in use, etc.). In theory it is possible to create a "frequency table" matching specific demon species to specific frequencies, and in fact much ink and time was spilled in the years following the invention of the Sensor, creating endless tables for "translating" specific demon signals. In the field Shadowhunters almost never have time to consult a table, and it is usually faster and easier for them to learn from experience to recognize demon types by sight. These tables are now considered mostly a historical curiosity. *But we have wasted your time by telling you about them anyway.*

These days Sensors are designed not to be manually tuned (though most can be so tuned if the user demands it) but to scan

31

up and down continuously for all demon activity and offer some educated guesses about the causes of any frequencies that appear. Modern Sensors may have mapping systems, proximity alarms, and other colorful features.

The Sensor often baffles new Shadowhunters, mostly because of its control buttons, which are labeled in angelic runes. This is done to allow the device to be used universally around the world, as the Shadowhunters do not share a single common language other than the language of Raziel and the Gray Book.

SENSORS THROUGH THE YEARS

THAT TITLE MAKES ME SLEEPY JUST LOOKING AT IT.

I have never in my life been bored enough to actually read this sidebar.

The first Sensor used as its warning mechanism a standard mechanical metronome, which in the proximity of demons would begin to clack rhythmically, its speed increasing as the demon and Sensor grew closer together. This metronome sat atop a large wooden box clasped in copper, the copper having been elaborately inscribed with Marks, and a variety of Marked and un-Marked mechanical works inside did the sensing and ran the metronome. The whole contraption sat atop a heavy cart with four wheels that had to be pushed around, since the metronome had to be kept level with the ground at all times and could easily be disrupted by unexpected movements. Various experiments took place through the early twentieth century to try to make the Sensor self-propelled and able to follow a Shadowhunter, patrol an area independently, and so on. These experiments never resulted in any usable innovation, and more often resulted in a dangerously mobile demon-powered cart that might at any moment charge the nearest Shadowhunter with unknown intent, clacking madly because of its extreme proximity to its own sensing apparatus. This failed branch of Sensor evolution fell away from the tree entirely in the 1960s when modern rune miniaturization magic made it possible to create Sensors that could be carried in a trouser pocket.

The Shadowhunter interested in its history can find older models displayed in libraries and museum collections of older Institutes.

Did you know? *No!* The Codex has a different definition of "interesting" than me

Interestingly, the standard runic labels on the Sensor were originally intended as a temporary measure. In his classic memoir of 1910, *A Whoops and a Bang: The Shadowhunter of the Modern Age,* Henry Branwell hypothesizes a single Mark that could be used to cause the buttons of a Sensor (or anything else) to appear in the native language of the person holding it. Such a Mark is not known to exist, but Branwell was at that time enthusiastically arguing for the use of warlock magic in collaboration with Nephilim Marks to create new and more complex effects, an unpopular position both then and now (although see the Grimoire, Chapter 6, for a discussion of the history of the Portal). This course of Branwell's experimentation, however, was disrupted when in 1914 he began a long collaboration with the Iron Sisters, the results of which remain secret to this day. The Mark of Translation remains uncreated, and the Sensor remains covered in runes whose meanings must be committed to memory.

SENSOR TECHNICAL SUPPORT
FREQUENTLY ASKED QUESTIONS

The Sensor is a complex tool, and many Shadowhunters struggle with the nuances of its use. Here we attempt to answer those questions that arise most frequently.

Yes, THAT IS WHAT "FREQUENTLY ASKED QUESTIONS" MEANS, THANK YOU.

Can the Sensor be modified to detect werewolves, vampires, and other Downworlders?

It cannot. The Sensor is attuned to the presence of demon energy; while Downworlders all have some demonic magic in them, they are not demons and do have normal human souls. Therefore they will not register on a Sensor.

Can the Sensor be modified to detect only certain kinds of demons?

Yes! This is a lesser-known but useful function of the Sensor that requires no modification. The buttons can be manipulated, using the Marks, to isolate only demons who match a certain set of qualities.

Can the Sensor be modified to detect a specific Greater Demon?

No.

Can the Sensor be modified to detect where I left some object?

No.

When will my Sensor support the Flash rune?

The Flash rune referred to here causes a burst of bright holy light, and rumors have existed for years that the Sensor was going to be modified to be able to successfully hold the Flash rune. Unfortunately, the Flash rune currently causes the Sensor's normal function to slow down and often stop working entirely. As yet, the only Sensors available do not support Flash, and only the Iron Sisters know whether they ever will.

Help, my Sensor's buttons are all labeled in runes.

Those are Marks.

I haven't learned these runes yet!

We might recommend a trick long known to Shadow-hunters, involving drawing your own labels on the Sensor buttons with a felt-tip marker.

My Sensor is vibrating!

That is within the normal bounds of Sensor operation. When a Sensor is overloaded with the proximity of demon energies, it will begin to vibrate with intensity. This was long considered a deficit in the design of Sensors, but the advent of modern technology has caused many Shadowhunters, especially those more familiar with the mundane world, to regard the vibration as a useful feature.

Unlike the mundane tools that vibrate, the Sensor can become so overloaded with demon energies that it can ignite and explode. Therefore, caution is advised.

My Sensor has vibrated so much that it has ignited and exploded.

You will, unfortunately, need to requisition a new Sensor from your Institute. Also, there is a tremendous quantity of demonic energy in your immediate vicinity. You must make sure to evaluate your immediate circumstances before trying to examine your Sensor; it is possible that you are about to be devoured by either a Greater Demon or a Portal to Hell.

So if you had a human who'd drunk a lot of Greater Demon blood when he was a baby, would he set off a Sensor?

Who would do such a terrible thing. Just hypothetically.

If you already know this guy, track him down! Sensors are for demons you don't already know personally!

Good point.

GOD, GET A ROOM, YOU TWO.

35

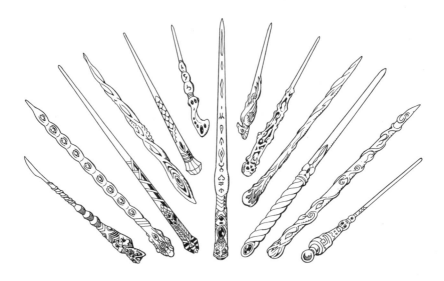

THE STELE

The stele (pronounced in English 'steh·lay) is listed here among the tools of the Shadowhunter but could just as easily be mentioned among weaponry; it is the fundamental tool of the Nephilim, the device by which Marks, our only magic, may be inscribed. An elaborate decorated stele is often the first tool given to a young Shadowhunter at the beginning of her studies.

The stele is a wandlike instrument, made of pure *adamas*. It is inert when not in use but when taken up glows and warms with the magic of the Marks. It is longer than modern writing instruments, usually a foot long or more, and as a result contemporary Shadowhunters will require practice to be able to draw runes with facility when using one.

All steles are functionally identical, but of course there is wide variation in their design. Many have handles inscribed with family crests and the like, some are studded with gems—the only requirement for a working stele is that it include an unbroken rod of *adamas* of at least a certain length. On the other end of the spectrum are the narrow practice steles given to child Nephilim to learn runic manuscription on sheets of parchment.

The first stele is believed to have been a rough oblong of *adamas* used by Jonathan Shadowhunter to inscribe the first Marks on his own skin. The stele designs have become refined over the years. Some scholars see a link between the stele and the Jewish *yad*, the ritual pointer used to avoid physically handling the parchment of the Torah when reading from it, but no direct connection can be made, although it is probable that the earliest Iron Sisters were inspired by such designs. REPRESENT!

Demons are not harmed by exposure to a stele, but they will typically recoil from one, as they will recoil from all *adamas*.

WITCHLIGHT STONES

One of the great secrets kept by the Iron Sisters is the precise manner by which *adamas* is extracted and purified from its ore. What we do know, however, is that the presence of *adamas* affects the rock from which it is extracted, and though it is simple rock, it gives off a pure white glow, as though reflecting the light inherent in the *adamas*. These "sister stones" of *adamas* are broken up and polished by Iron Sisters, and Marked to make their glow a property that can be turned on and off at the will of the Shadowhunter holding them. Most rune-stones are basic and interchangeable, and rarely do Shadowhunters get attached to a particular stone over any other. All Shadowhunters carry a witchlight stone, to remind them that light can be found even among the darkest shadows, and also to supply them with actual light when they are themselves literally among dark shadows.

The great advantage of witchlight stones is that their glow never fades or dissipates, for no fuel is being consumed in creating their light. Such a stone can, however, be destroyed by pulverizing it into dust, whereupon the angelic light absorbed into it will dissipate; thus one never finds "witchlight sand" or the like.

The largest single witchlight crystal in the world can be found in the Silent City in the form of the Angelic Colossus, a representation of the Triptych, the familiar motif of Raziel ascending from the water wielding the Mortal Instruments. The crystal stands roughly thirty feet tall, and it guards (and lights) the entrance to the Silent Brothers' living quarters. The Colossus is rarely seen by anyone other than the Silent Brothers, however, and those interested in large installations of witchlight are encouraged to visit the Institute of Cluj, where the renowned Vampire Arch forms the threshold to the Institute. For many years it was thought that humans infected with vampirism were sensitive to natural and holy light and would recoil from it; the Arch was built under the belief that it would protect the Institute from infected humans. We now know this not to be true, but the Arch remains as a symbol of the Cluj Institute's dedication to the Angel.

Or maybe they just like hurting vampires a lot.

Definitely that. Those Cluj guys are crazy.

See this is why you are a useful teacher I get the inside scoop.

I BELIEVE I MENTIONED SOMETHING ABOUT YOU TWO AND A ROOM A FEW PAGES AGO?

DISCUSSION QUESTIONS AND THINGS TO TRY

1. What's your everyday carry? What might you add to it to cover your new Shadowhunter responsibilities?

   Wallet, watch, phone, stele, pencils, sketchbook, waterproof fine-tip pen for inking, pencil sharpener, witchlight, mint lip balm.

   I HEAR CHAPPED LIPS ARE A LEADING CAUSE OF DEATH IN SHADOWHUNTERS. MY TURN! WALLET, WATCH, PHONE, BASS PICKS, PENS, NOTEBOOK, DICE OF VARIOUS KINDS, LITTLE CLOTH THINGIE TO CLEAN GLASSES WITH—EXCEPT I DON'T WEAR MY GLASSES ANYMORE, HUH. I GUESS I DON'T NEED TO CARRY THE CLOTH AROUND ANYMORE—SUPER-NERDY POCKETKNIFE. *Aaaand lip balm.*

   Don't even lie. You reek of strawberry right now.

2. What weapon might you like to specialize in? What about it draws your attention?

   ALAS! MY SECRET SHAME REVEALED!

   Go ahead, say "rapier wit." I know you want to.

   RAPIER WIT FINE YES THAT IS WHAT I WAS GOING TO SAY BECAUSE I AM SO FUNNY. *Poor Simon.*

   Anyway, I have no idea of an answer to this question, and frankly, Codex, this kind of question is the least of my problems right now. I would like to specialize in not being nearly killed yet again.

   I WOULD LIKE TO SPECIALIZE IN BEING AN IMMORTAL INVULNERABLE KILLING MACHINE WHO CRAVES THE BLOOD OF THE LIVING.

CHAPTER TWO

THE ARTS

COMBAT TRAINING

Once you have familiarized yourself with the tools of the Shadow-hunter, you must begin to learn the Shadowhunter's arts: combat, stealth, agility, endurance.

It surprises most new Shadowhunters to learn that there is no single set of skills that define us as warriors. We are found all over the globe, just as demons are found all over the globe. As such, there are as many varieties of Shadowhunter combat style as there are varieties in the mundane world. Typically you will undergo training in several different fighting styles, often selected from across human culture, and you will naturally find the styles that most appeal to you and with which you are most effective. You will be likely to study Western combat style, Eastern martial arts, and often stylized combat sports such as fencing or judo. There is a vast common ground of physical ability and prowess underlying almost all of these styles, and so as a new Shadowhunter you should expect to spend plenty of time on basic training to enhance your strength, speed, flexibility, and so on, before you have so much as picked up a weapon.

Marks may be used to enhance physical traits, but this is not typically done during training, and Marks cannot substitute for the muscle memory that the body learns through repetition and practice.

Our emphasis on learning from a wide range of sources is supported by a tradition whereby when Shadowhunters advance to majority at eighteen years old, they often travel and spend time in residence at an Institute well away from their home. There is great variation in local Shadowhunter cultures, both in philosophy and in specific techniques. Shadowhunters who have grown up in Idris are especially encouraged to travel, since the protected environment of Alicante may not prepare them for the harsh realities of the mundane world.

The newly made Shadowhunter, too, should seek to travel during her training, if at all possible. There is no obvious occasion to mark as there is with born Shadowhunters becoming adults, so talk with your Institute head or local Enclave about scheduling.

A PHILOSOPHY OF WAR

The first Shadowhunters, including Jonathan himself, dreamed of a world where someday their people would not need to be warriors. David the Silent, especially, loathed fighting and violence, and he wrote eloquently of the Nephilim's main mission to "discover Peace upon all the World." It's believed that the Silent Brothers were, in fact, founded with the primary mission of reversing the great evil acts of Sammael and Lilith, and closing our dimension again to demons. This philosophy continued to guide the Silent Brothers for hundreds of years. Brother Christopher de Sevilla could still write, in 1504, that the Nephilim's job was to "obsolete ourselves" by "driving the horde back and sealing the doors behind them."

The fact, however, is that a thousand years of work and research has brought us no closer to understanding how Sammael and Lilith accomplished their great Incursion, much less to discovering how it can be reversed. The thread of hope that the endless demonic horde could be turned back has frayed and is now so thin in Shadowhunter culture as to have nearly disappeared. Most believe today that if the

RECOMMENDED WEEKEND TRAINING
SCHEDULE FOR: CLARY FAIRCHILD

Just a proposed regimen for your weekend to keep you in good shape for next week. (Get ready for stick fighting!!!)

8-9 a.m.: Wake up. Eat breakfast (lean protein, light carb, NO CAFFEINE).

9-9:30 a.m.: Calisthenics @ home

9:30-10 a.m.: Yoga @ home

10 a.m.-12 p.m.: Language study (Greek, Latin)

12 p.m.-1 p.m.: Lunch

1 p.m.-3 p.m.: Intense cardio (running, probably)

3 p.m.-4 p.m.: Study demon weaknesses and appearances in textbook Demons, Demons, Demons.

4 p.m.-6 p.m.: Practice kata (your choice of martial arts school)

6 p.m.-7 p.m.: Dinner

7 p.m.-11 p.m.: Study (suggestions: history of faerie abductions, poisons and their antidotes, werewolf clan markings)

11 p.m.-12 a.m.: Free time!

12 a.m.: Sleep

WEEKEND TRAINING SCHEDULE FOR: ME

8 a.m.: Woke up.

9 a.m.: Woke up again; got up this time. Breakfast (bagel, scallion cream cheese, tomato, coffee w/milk). Calisthenics (walked briskly to deli and back).

10 a.m.–10:15 a.m.: Yoga. Very centering.

10:15 a.m.–11 a.m.: Language study (Looked through Latin textbook, watched last forty-five minutes of Gladiator. Fight scenes very inspiring. Took some notes.)

11 a.m.–12 p.m.: Took sketchbook to Prospect Park lawn. Simon brought lunch (noodles I like from place right by his house). Drew kids playing cricket on lawn. Studied cricket technique for potential application in combat. Drew gladiators playing cricket. Synthesis.

12 p.m.–1 p.m.: Lab: Interviewed vampire re: vampire history and culture, vampire combat techniques, etc. Very edifying.

1 p.m.–2 p.m.: Urban exploration (Took subway into Manhattan.)

2 p.m.–4 p.m.: Literary research (Visited comic book store, bought several volumes of long, illustrated study of medieval combat in Japan.)

4 p.m.: Healthy midafternoon snack (smoothie)

4 p.m.–7 p.m.: Watched research film in multiplex.

7 p.m.–9 p.m.: Dinner, tiny Korean place on Thirteenth, soup. (Soup is healthy!) Critiqued fight techniques seen in movie—very unrealistic.

9 p.m.–10 p.m.: Orienteering (subway home)

10 p.m.–12 a.m.: Talked on phone with primary Shadowhunter trainer, updated him on status. Planned training regimen for following day. Exchanged positive affirmations.

12 a.m.–2 a.m.: Read illustrated study of medieval Japanese combat. Cultural exchange with vampire re: illustrated study, vampire's current boredom. Fell asleep, practiced difficult "balance phone on face" technique for indefinite period of time before it fell onto the floor and woke me up.

2 a.m.: A refreshing, well-earned sleep.

demonic tide is to be turned, it will be Heaven's doing, not ours. Our role is to stand behind the open gates and turn them back one by one. And so we fight.

SUBJECTS OF NEPHILIM STUDY

This Codex intends to provide you, the newly minted Shadowhunter, with the basic knowledge you will need to survive and understand your new world and your new people. We cannot possibly provide a full course of training in these pages, and mere written instruction, without the help of a skilled instructor who could not only demonstrate techniques but evaluate your abilities, would be a disservice to the training you deserve.

Instead we here provide the outlines of a general course of Shadowhunter training, along with touchstone goals for beginners, for more intermediate students, and for those seeking true expertise. It can be difficult for new Shadowhunters to understand their own training progress. We do not have ranks, promotions, "belts," levels, merit badges, or anything of the kind. Most of your fellow Nephilim have lived in our warrior culture their whole lives, and the qualities of the well-tempered Shadowhunter have been part of their upbringing. These suggestions therefore should not be taken as rigid requirements but rather as guidelines that may help you understand your progress as you train.

One final note for the especially ambitious Shadowhunter: No one can be an expert at all things. As you train, one of your goals will be to find those elements of Shadowhunter life that you wish to pursue more closely, because of either your natural aptitude in them or your interest in deeper study. All Shadowhunters should first aim to achieve at least beginner competence in all of these categories before seeking more advanced study.

MONOMACHIA (HAND-TO-HAND COMBAT)

Beginner: Basic competence ("black belt" equivalent) in at least one Eastern martial art or Western fighting tradition. Ability to reliably fend off two to three simultaneous attackers.

Intermediate: Competence in three to five mundane fighting traditions. Ability to reliably fend off five to eight simultaneous attackers.

Expert: Competence in more than ten mundane fighting traditions. Ability to reliably fend off an arbitrarily large army of demons.

RANGED-MISSILE COMBAT

Beginner: Competence with standard set of ranged weapons— longbow, crossbow, sling, thrown daggers, javelins, big heavy rocks.

Intermediate: Competence with above while blindfolded.

Expert: Competence with above while blindfolded and lying down.

STEALTH

Beginner: Ability to pass undetected through darkened alley or room.

Intermediate: Ability to pass undetected through darkened alley or room filled with small breakable objects precariously balanced atop other breakable objects.

Expert: Ability to pass undetected through open terrain in broad daylight.

BLENDING AND CONCEALMENT

Beginner: Ability to pass as a mundane in a typical public scenario ("driving a car," "shopping for food," etc.). Please see *Mundanes Do the Darndest Things*, 1988 edition, in your local Institute library, for suggestions.

Intermediate: Ability to pass as a mundane at a small cocktail party or reception.

Expert: Ability to pass as a mundane in the midst of a mundane demonic cult performing a human sacrifice.

AGILITY AND GRACE

Beginner: Basic competence at acrobatics, tumble, trapeze, gymnastics, etc.

Intermediate: Competence at above skills while wearing thirty kilograms of gear and several heavy weapons.

Expert: Competence at above skills while wearing thirty kilograms of gear, several heavy weapons, a blindfold, and iron manacles.

ENDURANCE

Beginner: Competence at improvised survival skills in typical harsh environments (e.g., high desert, drifting ice floe).

Intermediate: Competence with above in extreme environments (e.g., inside a building that is on fire, free-falling from an airplane at high cruising altitude, in outer space, in Hell).

Expert: Ability to withstand torture by Greater Demon while in above harsh or extreme environments.

TRACKING

Beginner: Knowledge of tracking runes; ability to identify telltale signs of animal or demon activity and maintain pursuit.

Intermediate: Ability to maintain pursuit while also evading similar pursuit by different animal or demon.

Expert: Ability to maintain pursuit while in harsh or extreme environments (see Endurance, above).

ORIENTEERING

Beginner: Intuitive grasp of altitude, cardinal direction, time of day, weather conditions, etc.

Intermediate: Ability to find way to known safe location when dropped into arbitrary environment.

Expert: Ability to find way to known safe location when dropped into extreme or harsh environment (see above).

OBSERVATION AND DEDUCTION

Beginner: Basic forensics knowledge; ability to "read" the scene of a crime and reconstruct events there with high probability of accuracy.

Intermediate: Ability to reliably identify revealing details of a scene that mundane law enforcement would typically overlook.

Expert: As above, but while blindfolded.

LANGUAGES

Beginner: Knowledge of several mundane languages, preferably a mixture of living languages spoken near your geographical base and ancient languages used in religious writings (e.g., Sanskrit, Hebrew, ancient Greek, Sumerian).

Intermediate: Knowledge of the above and at least two demonic languages.

Expert: Knowledge of the above, at least four demonic languages, and ability to intuit basic meanings from written or spoken language never encountered before.

DIPLOMACY

Beginner: Ability to talk your way out of being eaten by a demon or killed by angry Downworlder horde.

A Quick Evaluation of Me and 48 My Friends By the Above Scale:

Alec: Intermediate, Expert, Intermediate, Intermediate, Expert, Intermediate, Intermediate, Beginner, Intermediate, Beginner, Intermediate.

Isabelle: Expert, Intermediate, Beginner, Beginner, Expert, Expert, Intermediate, Intermediate, Intermediate, Intermediate, Beginner.

Me: Beginner, Beginner, Beginner, Expert (I am very good at blending in with the mundane world!), Serious Beginner, Beginner,

Intermediate: Ability to talk your way out of being eaten by Greater Demon or killed by angry Downworlder political leadership. *Intermediate, Intermediate, Beginner, Expert (I am counting runes here, okay?),*

Expert: Ability to talk your way out of being eaten by Greater Demon or killed by angry Downworlder political leadership, and to convince said demon or Downworlders that letting you go was their idea.

Expert (at least compared to the rest of this group).

WHY DON'T NEPHILIM USE FIREARMS?

Guns are rarely used by Shadowhunters because, for our purposes, they normally do not work correctly. Etching Marks into the metal of a gun or bullet prevents gunpowder from successfully igniting. Considerable research has been done into this problem, with little success. The prevailing theories today prefer an alchemical explanation, contrasting the heavenly source of our Marks with the demonically allied brimstone and saltpeter that make up classic gunpowder, but this explanation does not, unfortunately, hold much weight. Demonic runes have the same impeding effect on guns as our own Marks, and the problem remains even with the use of modern propellants, which do not contain these supposedly "demonic" materials. This remains one of the great unexplained mysteries of runic magic, and researchers continue to pursue explanations and solutions to this day.

Me: Expert, Intermediate, Expert, Expert, Expert, Expert, Expert, Expert, Expert, Beginner.

Me: Vampire, Vampire, Vampire, Vampire, Vampire, Vampire, Vampire, Vampire, Vampire, Vampire, Vampire.

49

Guns can, of course, be successfully used to harm vampires and (with silver bullets) werewolves, but shots must be made with pinpoint accuracy. The risk of collateral damage and the difficulty of scoring a direct hit, combined with the understanding that Shadowhunter weapons will be overwhelmingly used to fight demons rather than Downworlders, has led to a general rejection of firearms as part of the Shadowhunter arsenal.

Finally, it is to the advantage of the Nephilim to have our weapons forged and built by the Iron Sisters as much as possible. Modern gunsmithing involves elaborate industrial machining that our traditional weapons don't require, and if we were to have the Iron Sisters forge firearms, that would drastically change the Iron Sisters' need for resources and equipment.

THE TRADITION OF THE *PARABATAI*

> Whither thou goest, I will go;
> Where thou diest, will I die, and there will I be buried:
> The Angel do so to me, and more also,
> If aught but death part thee and me.
> —The Oath of the Parabatai

The tradition of the *parabatai* goes back to the beginnings of the Shadowhunters; the first *parabatai* were Jonathan Shadowhunter himself and his companion, David. They in turn were inspired by their coincident namesakes, from the biblical tale of Jonathan and David:

50

"And it came to pass . . . , that the soul of Jonathan was knit with the soul of David, and Jonathan loved him as his own soul. . . . Then Jonathan and David made a covenant, because he loved him as his own soul."
—1 Samuel 18:1–3

Out of that tradition Jonathan Shadowhunter created the *parabatai*, and codified the ceremony into Law.

David the Silent was not at first a Silent Brother (See Excerpts from *A History of the Nephilim*, Appendix A, for more details). At first there were no Silent Brothers; earliest Nephilim hoped that their more difficult and mystical roles could be integrated into their warrior selves. Only as time passed did it become clear that the work of David would take him ever toward the angelic and farther and farther from his physical form. David and his followers set down their weapons, exchanging them for a life of mystical contemplation and the pursuit of wisdom.

Before this time, however, Jonathan and David fought side by side as the first *parabatai*. Tradition tells us that the ritual they performed, where they took of each other's blood and spoke the words of the oath and inscribed the runes of binding upon each other, was the second-to-last time that David was known to shed human tears. The last time was the moment when the *parabatai* bond was broken, as David took the Marks that made him the first Silent Brother. This is a bromance of very heavy-duty proportions. You have no idea.

Today *parabatai* must be bonded in childhood; that is, before either has turned eighteen years old. They are not merely warriors who fight together; the oaths that newly made *parabatai* take in front of the Council include vows to lay down one's life for the other, to travel where the other travels, and indeed, to be buried in the same place. The Marks of *parabatai* are then put upon them, which enable them to draw on each other's strength in battle. They are able to sense each other's life force; Shadowhunters who have lost their *parabatai* describe being able to feel the life leave their partner. In addition, Marks made by one *parabatai* upon another are stronger than other Marks, and there are Marks that only *parabatai* can use, because they draw on the partners' doubled strength.

The only bond forbidden to the *parabatai* is the romantic bond. These bonded pairs must maintain the dignity of their warrior bond and must not allow it to transform into the earthly love we call Eros. The late Middle Ages were littered with Shadowhunter-troubadours' songs of the forbidden love of *parabatai* pairs and the tragedies that befell them. The warnings are not merely of heartache and betrayal but of magical disaster, impossible to prevent, when *parabatai* become romantically linked.

Like the marriage bond, the *parabatai* bond is broken, normally, only by the death of one of the members of the partnership. The binding can also be cut in the rare occurrence that one of the partners becomes a Downworlder or a mundane. Per above, the bond dissolves naturally if one of the partners becomes a Silent Brother or Iron Sister: The Marks of transformation that new oblates take are among the most powerful that exist and overwhelm and dissolve the *parabatai* Marks of binding just as they overwhelm and dissolve more ordinary warrior's Marks.

A Shadowhunter may choose only one *parabatai* in his lifetime and cannot perform the ritual more than once. Most Shadowhunters never have any *parabatai* at all; if you, newmade Nephilim, find yourself with one, consider it a great blessing.

—— HOW TO REPORT A DEMON ——

- If you are not sure you can handle the demon yourself, do not engage it in battle or even in conversation.
- Remember such things as the number of demons, exact location, their current activity.
- If you know the demon's species (or name, in the case of a Greater Demon), report it; if you *don't* know the demon's species, remember possible identifying features such as:
  » Skin color (gray, green, purple-black, iridescent) and texture (scales, hide, bony spikes, fur)
  » Presence of slime, color of slime
  » Number of eyes, mouths, noses, arms, legs, heads
  » Size (compare to other things of similar size rather than trying to estimate actual measurement—e.g., "about as big as a grizzly bear")
  » Noises (languages spoken, high-pitched voice versus low-pitched voice)

» Gender markings (very rare except with Greater Demons)
» Noticeable strengths (eats rocks or metal, ability to cling to walls and ceilings, etc.) and weaknesses (sensitive to being harmed by frostbite, compulsive need to count individual grains of spilled rice, overweening pride)
» Obvious sources of physical danger: fangs, talons, claws, spines, constricting body, acid blood, prehensile tongue, etc.

· Bring your thorough report to your local Institute, which will evaluate the threat and decide on next steps. You can assist by searching for the demon you've seen in *Deutsch's Demonfinder*, the definitive resource cataloguing demons based on their physical characteristics. (It is, however, quite possible that the Institute already knows of the demon you're reporting, in which case the investigation may be quite short.)

CHAPTER THREE

Bestiaire Part I:
DEMONOLOGIE

Demons, the great trespassers into our universe, are the reason why the Nephilim exist. They are the shadows that we hunt. Though our work managing and maintaining the careful balance among Downworlders and mundanes often feels like the majority of our responsibility, it is secondary. It is the work we do when we are not fighting demons. The primary task of the Shadowhunter, the mission granted us by Raziel, is to eliminate the demon scourge by returning the demons, once and for all, to the Void from whence they came.

—— WHAT ARE DEMONS? ——

The very word "demon" is problematic. Its etymology in English has nothing to do with evil spirits at all; it is used to describe these creatures only because of translation confusions in the early days of Christianity, many years before the Nephilim began. We use the word "demons" to describe the creatures we fight because Jonathan Shadowhunter used the word, based on his own religious history. Most human belief systems have some concept that represents what we call demons: Persian daevas, Hindu asuras, Japanese oni. To keep terminology uncomplicated, we refer to them as demons, as do most Nephilim.

Demons are not living beings in the sense that we usually understand. They are alien to our universe and are not sustained by the same kind of forces that sustain us. Demons do not have souls; instead, they are powered by a roiling demon energy, a vitalizing

57

spark that maintains their form in our dimension. When demons die, this energy is separated from its physical body, and that body will be yanked quickly back into its home dimension. To human eyes, this disappearance can take many forms, depending on the species of demon. Some explode into dust, some fade from view, some crumple into themselves. In all cases, however, no remnant of the demon's physical self remains in our world. (Warlock rituals exist that can "preserve" demonic physicality in our world, allowing one to keep, say, a vial of demon blood without its vanishing when its demon source is dispatched.)

WHAT DO DEMONS WANT WITH OUR WORLD? WHY DO THEY COME HERE?

We do not really know. Nephilim folklore says that demons are originally *from* our world, before they were banished (see Excerpts from A *History of the Nephilim*, Appendix A), so perhaps they are seeking to take it back for themselves. On the other hand, our stories also tell us that the demons were destructive and wicked from the beginning—that is why they were banished. So they may instead represent the spirit of evil in our world, in some fashion.

At an individual level, demons seem to come to our world in order to wreak havoc. Sometimes they come in search of power— power over other creatures, more powerful magic, and the like— but that power seems to have no ultimate purpose beyond its own existence, other than to wreak more havoc upon our world.

Many have argued for more philosophical origins of the demons' hate for our world—that they hate our ability to create, for instance, which they lack. This argument is often used to explain why demons create warlocks: It is the only act of creation of which they are capable, and even that they must accomplish by stealing our own act of creation from us.

But we must, for now, throw up our hands and admit that it remains a mystery why demons come to our world. All we can say for sure is that they are here to do us violence, and that they have no interest in truces or treaties.

WHAT DO DEMONS "REALLY" LOOK LIKE? DO THEY LOOK LIKE UGLY MONSTERS EVEN WHEN IN THEIR OWN DIMENSION?

The relationship of demons' bodies in our world to their "reality" in their own is a secret we may never discover. We believe that demons have no choice about the physical form they take in our world, but other than that, their true form is a mystery. We do not know if terms like "appearance" even apply in the Void from whence they come. One popular theory holds that when a demon travels to a dimension, a body is created for that demon that can survive in that dimension, and that this is the reason that demons are the only creatures that can move freely between worlds. This is mere conjecture, of course.

HOW DO I RECOGNIZE A DEMON IN THE WILD?

Recognizing demons, unless they are shapeshifters, is normally not difficult. Demons always take on monstrous forms in our world, and can usually be discerned by the uncanny, nauseating feeling that billows around them like a dark aura. In the rare cases of uncertainty, positive identification can be made via the demon's violent reaction to holy items and places or via a Sensor's violent reaction to the demon.

In addition to their general hideousness, demons often carry with them a scent of death that can be very strong. Shadowhunters asked to describe it usually reach for terms like "rotting," "spoiled," "brimstone," "burning hair," and the like. The effect can be debilitating to the unprepared Shadowhunter.

I AM ACTUALLY FEELING KIND OF BAD FOR DEMONS HERE.

IS THAT WRONG? *Yes.*

WHAT IS THAT DISGUSTING BLACK LIQUID THAT APPEARS WHEN YOU CUT THEM?

Like other living creatures, demons' bodies are kept fresh by a vital fluid, but this is not the usual red blood of our world. Instead, they contain a supernatural ichor. The term "ichor" refers originally to the golden blood of angels, and comes from the ancient Greek word for the blood of their gods. Demon blood is also ichor, but as it is infused with demon energies, it is black and viscous, thinner than blood but totally opaque. Ichor is not dangerous to touch, but it is somewhat toxic to humans if it gets into the blood via a wound or other means. It is unlikely to harm any Shadowhunter who has the usual range of protective Marks, but care should be taken.

CAN DEMONS SPEAK HUMAN LANGUAGES?

Most common demons cannot speak human languages. A good number of species are, however, able to parrot human speech that they have heard. This is often a sign that a demon has been summoned rather than coming to our world on its own; the demon will be heard to repeat, often obsessively, words and phrases spoken to it by the summoner.

There are a number of demon languages—possibly an infinite number of them—but a number that we have identified and that warlocks and, more rarely, Shadowhunters interested in demon research may learn. The two most common are known to demon philologists as Cthonic and Purgatic. It is worthwhile to at least be able to recognize these two languages in their written and spoken forms, and perhaps to memorize a few frequently used phrases, such as "Hello," "Good-bye," "I am a Nephilim," "In the name of Raziel I abjure thee," "Begone, fiend," and so on.

DO DEMONS POSSESS PEOPLE?

Despite the mundane obsession with demons taking possession of their bodies, actual demon possession is very rare and requires a very powerful Greater Demon. This is lucky, because it is one of the most powerful magics that demons possess. Usually the only way the connection between the possessor and the possessed can be broken is by killing the demon, which more often than not kills the hapless mundane victim as well. If you encounter a possession, *do not* try to handle the situation on your own. Do not try to negotiate with the possessed as if they are political hostages. The possessed are not merely corrupted by demonic influence but are fully controlled. They become like passengers in their own bodies, able to experience everything that the demon is doing but unable to exert any will to act independently at all. (Mercifully, the possessed usually retain no memories of their actions while inhabited.) You may restrain the victim, preferably with help from other Shadowhunters, and then you should contact the Silent Brothers and allow them to remove the subject to the Silent City, where they will perform magics that you are better off not witnessing.

61

WHY ARE DEMONS SO EAGER TO DESTROY US?

It's believed that demons have an intrinsic hatred of us as a result of their envy of the life of our dimension. Theirs, as far as we can tell, is a dead dimension, a dimension devoid of life, and they desire to consume us and our world to take that which they themselves do not (or, perhaps, no longer) have. Demons are able to sense the presence of life nearby; in fact, they will often use this sense to track down their prey.

> **DID YOU KNOW?**
> One of the great unsung heroes of the Nephilim is Gregory Hans, a seventeenth-century Silent Brother who discovered the correct combination of Marks to both enhance a Nephilim's senses and exclude the smell of demons from that enhancement. Generations of Shadowhunters thank him. (Note that under standard demonic glamour, those who are susceptible cannot smell a demon any more than they can hear or see one. All the senses, thankfully, are negated.)

—— HOW DO WE KILL THEM? ——

The most important weakness of demons is, of course, their vulnerability to angelic power and heavenly fire. Like the Downworlders they brought into being, they cannot easily be harmed by normal earthly weapons, or at least not permanently harmed. For this reason you will find even the most basic Shadowhunter weapons to be Marked to strengthen them against demons, and you will find the seraph blade (see Treasury, Chapter 1) to be the most important of your tools in combat.

In addition to being repelled by direct seraphic energy, most demons can be warded off with holy symbols of all kinds. Very powerful demons, however, such as Greater Demons, may be caused only discomfort by the presence of holy symbols, rather than actual harm, so a Shadowhunter should not depend exclusively on these symbols to protect themselves.

Like vampires, demons cannot stand the direct force of sunlight upon their bodies. Note that—just as in the case of vampires—this does not mean that demons are not active during daylight hours. They can stand our artificial lights with no ill effects. And unlike vampires, who often attempt to live undetected among mundanes, demons have no need to pretend to tolerate sunlight. It is possible to destroy a demon with light, but the Shadowhunter will need to somehow entrap the demon in a situation where sunlight cannot be escaped, which can be difficult. A seraph blade to the throat or heart is usually a more reliable attack.

Finally, one great advantage that we have in our fight against demons is that they are unable to perceive the difference between mundanes and Shadowhunters, and unable to sense the working of angelic magic. This enables us to hide from them using glamours until such time as we are ready to fight them. Demons can, however, detect the presence of other demons and Downworlders.

This section summarized for your convenience:
We don't know a thing about either of these.

THE VOID AND THE DEMON CITY OF PANDEMONIUM

Well, that is a time saver, thanks.

We know little about the Void, the home of demonkind. Many names have been used in literature to refer to the home of the demons—all mundane religious terms for Hell, and other abstract terms such as "Chaos" and "Abyss," for example—but in

63

modern times we have settled on "Void" as both descriptive and ecumenical, and, oddly enough, the Greater Demons who have manifested in our world in modern times have also used the term.

The geography of the Void remains a mystery to us. It often appears that demons have no real homes and are present everywhere at all times. One can, for instance, summon any demon for whom a summoning ritual is known, and all of these demons will appear reliably and in roughly the same amount of time, whatever kind of demon and wherever the summoner may be. On the other hand, certain species of demons tend to "naturally" occur in certain parts of our world—the Rakshasas of the Indian subcontinent, for example, or the Gorgons of Greece. Plenty of theories have been advanced as to why this might be, but the fact is that we do not understand why certain demons have an affinity for certain locations. The fact that some demons do have an affinity for a location is to our advantage, though. Those Shadowhunters posted in certain places will become experts in fighting particular kinds of demons and for the most part will not have to know everything about all demons but will be able to locally specialize.

One may generally assume that the number of different demons in the Void is, for all intents and purposes, infinite. At the very least, it's believed that there are hundreds upon hundreds of millions of different types, and while Shadowhunters have fought demons for the entirety of our thousand-year history, it's unlikely that we've encountered more than the tiniest percentage of them. It's speculated that there are many demons who are incapable of manifesting themselves materially in our world at all.

A constant in our communication with those demons who can speak human language is their references to the city of Pandemonium, the supposed great nexus of demons at the center of the Void, if a void can be said to have a center. No human has, of course, ever visited that city and returned to tell the tale, so it is impossible to make any definite statements about it and what it is like, or even to say whether it can be described as a physical entity in the manner of our cities at all. About the only thing we can say about Pandemonium definitely is that it is very, very large— staggeringly larger than any of our human cities, and possibly larger and more populous than Earth. Research on Pandemonium has been limited, largely because most Nephilim consider that there are enough demons present in our world without going to find still more of them.

DEMONS VERSUS GREATER DEMONS

We do not know if there are actually "Greater Demons."

There are specific demons that we refer to as Greater Demons, and they have some aspects in common: human-scale intelligence, personalities, names, and an inability to be permanently destroyed by us with any weapon available. We know this because of a long recorded history of Greater Demons who have been "killed," only to return later, intact and unharmed. Void Theory tells us that the destruction of the Greater Demon's physical body sends the Greater Demon snapping back to the spaces in the Void, where its ethereal body exists. There the Greater Demon must spend time carefully accruing power in order to rebuild its physical form.

But it's important also to remember that this is mostly speculation. It may be the case, for instance, that no demons, Greater or otherwise, can be permanently killed by us, but since we can't discern individuals among the demons that have subhuman intelligence, we cannot tell if a demon we believe we have killed actually returns later. Attempts have been made at various points in history to "tag" individual demons for tracking, usually with terrible results. Killing demons is difficult enough; catching a small number alive in order to tag and track them has proven impossible.

It is possible, therefore, that "Greater Demon" simply means "any demon with humanlike intelligence," rather than the term indicating some firmer distinction between Greater Demons and regular demons. More research will be needed to discover the truth; luckily, the endless torrent of hideous un-life from beyond the Void shows no sign of slowing, and research material will likely never be in short supply.

— DEMONS, DEMONS, DEMONS —

Now with additional demons!

I. SOME GREATER DEMONS

LILITH

Unlike her dark consort, Sammael, Lilith is still alive and has been known to appear on Earth. Pray that you never meet her.

Lilith is known by many names, even when considering only the Jewish tradition from which most of her folklore is sourced. This does not count the many other entities in other mythological traditions that are similar in form or function and may or may not be the same demon. Lilith's other names in Jewish folklore include: Satrina, Abito, Amizo, Izorpo, Kokos, Odam, Ita, Podo, Eilo, Patrota, Abeko, Kea, Kali, Batna, Talto, and Partash.

Jewish tradition says that for her disobedience she was punished by being made unable to bear children. Many versions of the tale paint an even more brutal picture in which Lilith actually *is* capable of birthing infants, but all of them die upon birth. As such she is associated with the harming and weakening of human babies, and much of our knowledge of Lilith comes from Jewish mystical tradition designed to protect newborns from Lilith's influence, with amulets and incantations.

SAMMAEL

Apart from his foundational role in the Incursion, not much is known about Sammael. He is thought to have been the great Serpent by which humanity was tempted and fell from grace. But his physical shape is a mystery, for Sammael has not been seen on Earth in many hundreds of years.

Traditional tales state that for his crime of softening the veils between the human world and the Void, he was hunted and murdered by the archangel Michael, commander of the armies of Heaven. This story comes to us through mundane religious tradition, but is often repeated and is clearly believed by the demons of Pandemonium themselves. Since Sammael has not been seen in our world for so long a time, no rituals survive to summon him.

ABBADON

The Demon of the Abyss. His are the empty places between the worlds. His is the wind and the howling darkness. He is a nine-foot-tall rotting human skeleton. *He is a real jerk.*

AZAZEL

Lieutenant of Hell and Forger of Weapons. Like most of the greatest

67

of Greater Demons, he was an angel at one time. He is said to have taught humanity how to make weapons in the times before history, where previously weapons making had been knowledge held only by angels. This great transgression caused him to fall and become a demon. The irony of a demon being responsible for giving humanity the knowledge necessary to fight against demons is not lost on the Nephilim; we assume that it is not lost on Azazel himself either. As the Book of Enoch has it, "And the whole earth has been corrupted by the works that were taught by Azazel. To him ascribe all sin."

HUNGER

The demon known as Hunger is an obese devil-like humanoid figure covered in hard, bony scales and a variety of chomping fang-lined mouths all over his body. Hunger is made to devour everything he encounters, usually in as messy and grotesque a fashion as possible.

MARBAS

A blue demon, half again the size of a man, covered in overlapping blue scales, with a long yellowish tail with a stinger on the end. Scarlet eyes, lizard's features, and a flat snakelike snout.

MRS. DARK

A large creature of hard, stonelike skin, apparently female (although what gender means in the realm of demons is unclear). She is horned, with twisted limbs and clawed hands. She can also be identified by her glowing yellow eyes and her triple row of mouths lined with greenish fangs. She is of the Eidolon (see separate entry on page 70).

II. SOME COMMON DEMONS

BEHEMOTH

The Behemoth is a formless monstrosity of a demon. It is roughly oblong and could be described as sluglike in its movements, but with less coherence of shape. It is large, much larger than a human, and slimy. Double rows of teeth line the length of its body. The Behemoth devours everything in its path, including people.

DRAGON

Dragon demons are the closest thing in the modern world to the ancient myths of dragons. They are large, flying, fire-breathing lizards, and are quite intelligent. They come in a variety of shapes and colors. They are formidable foes; luckily, Shadowhunters are likely to never encounter them, since they are almost extinct. They are not to be confused with Vetis demons, which are like dragons but are not Dragons.

DREVAK

Shadowhunters know well the appearance of Drevaks, weak demons in frequent use by Greater Demons or evil warlocks as spies or messengers. They are smooth, white, and larval, resembling a giant version of a mundane grub or maggot. They are blind and do their tracking by scent.

Their shapelessness and lack of intelligence does not mean they are not dangerous; instead of teeth their mouths contain poisonous spines, which can be very dangerous if they break off and stick in the skin of a victim. Normal treatments for demon venom apply here.

DU'SIEN

The Du'sien is one of the lesser-known shape-shifting, or Eidolon, demon species (see below). Its true appearance is abstract, like an irregular blob of greenish-gray jelly with a small glowing black core. They cannot mimic other creatures with the detail that many Eidolon can, and their command of human language is weak. They are thus often found disguised as "generic humans," members of a crowd, rather than impersonating specific individuals.

EIDOLON

"Eidolon" is not the name for a specific species of demon. Rather, it is a comprehensive term for a variety of shape-shifting demon species. Shape-shifting demons come in many different original shapes, and many different sizes and strengths. Since there are dozens of these species, Shadowhunters typically use the term "Eidolon" to refer to shape-shifting demons in general. It is, in other words, usually more useful to note a demon's shape-shifting ability than the minor details of their original form.

Eidolon demons make up the majority of demon parents of warlocks, for obvious reasons. (See the "Warlocks" section of Part II of this Bestiaire for an explanation if the reasons are not obvious to you.)

In addition to the danger posed by their nearly perfect ability to camouflage themselves, Eidolon also have a marked advantage over other demon species: When shifted into the form of a human, they are somewhat protected from the destructive light of the sun. A shifted Eidolon demon still cannot stand in direct sunlight but can endure the diffused light coming through heavy clouds, fog, rain, and so on, with only minor discomfort.

FACEMELTER

Self-explanatory.

HELLHOUND

A demonic corruption of the dog, just as many demons are corruptions of the forms of men and women. Typically hellhounds appear as vicious canines much larger than any mundane dog, with red eyes, coarse black wirelike fur, and a murderous temperament. They have a similar intelligence to mundane dogs and are used by demons for similar purposes—tracking and hunting. (Obviously there are many uses for mundane dogs, such as herding and companionship, that hellhounds are never used for, since demons are incapable of concepts such as companionship.) Like with dogs, hellhounds' jaws are their most dangerous weapons, but unlike with dogs, their tails end in a set of spiked nail-like protrusions, similar to a mace.

HYDRA

A medium-size multiheaded demon, vicious but not intelligent. Known for its multiple heads, at least three but often many more. The Hydra can be distinguished from other multiheaded demons by its animalistic intelligence level, the presence of heads on stalks, and its blindness—the Hydra cannot see normally and relies on sound, scent, and its sheer number of large mouths to catch its prey.

IBLIS

The Iblis demon is corporeal but not of solid form. Instead it has the appearance of a figure about the size and shape of a human but made of a roiling, fast-moving black smoke. In the part of its vapor that represents its head, it looks out onto our world through yellow burning eyes.

IMP

The common Imp is a small humanoid with the characteristics of a typical Western devil—horns, forked tail, et cetera. They

71

are not very dangerous individually but can become a problem when encountered in swarms of more than two hundred, as is occasionally reported.

DJINN

Djinn are mentioned here because they are often incorrectly believed to be demons. They are not; they are faeries.

KAPPA

A reptilian water demon covered in a protective carapace and with a protruding beak, but otherwise the size and rough shape of a human ten-year-old child. Fond of leaping from the water to drag unwitting mundanes to their deaths.

KURI

These are spider demons, large and shiny black, with eight pincer-tipped arms, and fangs extending from their eye sockets.

MOLOCH

Somewhat confusingly, the name "Moloch" refers both to a Greater Demon known as one of the most fearsome demon warriors, a being of smoke and oil, and also to a species of lesser demons ("Molochs") that are minions and foot soldiers of the Greater Demon Moloch. Individuals of the species are man-size, dark, and made of thick roiling oil, with arms but only a formless liquid appendage instead of legs. Their primary weapon is the flames that stream from their empty eye sockets, and they are usually seen in large numbers rather than in isolation.

ONI

Human-size demons with green skin, wide mouths, and horns upon their heads.

RAHAB

These are large bipedal demons, somewhat lizardlike in appearance and movement. They are blind, with a line of teeth where their eyes should be, and a regular mouth, this one fanged and tusked, in a more usual place on their faces. They have a narrow, whiplike tail edged with razor-sharp bone. Their talons and teeth are, of course, sharp and dangerous, but their most threatening weapon is the bulb-shaped stinger on the end of their long, forked tongue.

RAUM

The Raum is an intimidating and dangerous demon, not capable of speech, but somewhat clever as an opponent nonetheless. Raums are about the size of a man but possess white, scaled skin, bulging black eyes without pupils, a perfectly circular mouth, and tentacles for arms. These tentacles are the Raum's most dangerous weapon; they are tipped with red suckers, each of which contains a circle of tiny needlelike teeth.

RAVENER

The Ravener is a classic monstrosity: a long, squamous black body with a long domed skull like an alligator's. Unlike on an alligator, its eyes are in an insectile cluster on the top of its head. It has a vicious, barbed whip tail and a thick, flat snout. Raveners possess sharp fanged teeth, which envenomate their prey with a deadly toxin. In time the poison will burn away all of the life of the victim, leaving only ash behind. The toxin is particularly terrible even among demon venoms, and there we are talking about a category that includes the poison of the Facemelter demon. (See "Facemelter," page 70.)

73

SHAX

These demons are known for their keen sense of smell and are sometimes summoned by warlocks to use in tracking a missing person. They must be carefully controlled, however; they are brood parasites and reproduce by wounding a victim and then laying their eggs in the still-living victim's skin.

VERMITHRALL

Most Shadowhunters will incorrectly tell you that the Vermithrall is a monstrous lumbering mass made up of thousands of writhing worms. In fact the Vermithrall are the individual worms themselves. They do, however, collect into colonies in the shape of a humanoid and attack as a unified single entity. Worse, worms separated from the main body will endeavor to rejoin it, making it very hard to permanently kill a Vermithrall.

VETIS

They are not to be confused with Dragon demons, which they somewhat resemble but are unrelated to. They are gray and scaly, with overlong serpentine arms and an elongated but humanoid body. Like Dragons, they are known for hoarding valuables; unlike Dragons, they do not have any understanding of what is valuable and what is dross, and their lairs are more closely reminiscent of large rats' nests than treasure chambers.

MUNDANE DEMONIC CULTS

Through history there have been any number of pathetic, misguided groups of mundanes who have built small cults around the worship of a particular demon or group of demons. Most of these cults are of little interest to Nephilim and serve only to clutter and confuse demonic histories, since they are based around demons that are merely imagined or invented.

Nevertheless, a minority of these demon cults have successfully raised weak minor demons. These stories usually end with the cult improperly binding the demon and the demon immediately killing all of the cult's members. In a small number of cases, a successful demon cult has endured for a short time, with the demon served by the cult members and asking little in return. These cults inevitably fade after a generation or two and are of little concern to us historically, but they may cause local trouble and require Shadowhunter intervention.

Mundane members of demon cults are often barely human by the time that intervention is needed. Their worshipped demon is likely to have consumed their humanity for fuel, to maintain and strengthen itself. This leaves behind mere shells of humans, their physical bodies in active decay and their souls worn down to a constant animalistic rage. This state is considered irreversible; killing these demon-degraded mundanes is considered an act of mercy and is thus within the bounds of the Law.

Cults have existed to serve Greater Demons, but there is little evidence that any of these have ever successfully summoned the subject of their worship. If they have, the likelihood is that they were immediately annihilated and no record exists of them to teach us of their folly.

THE DEMON POX

Astriola, or demon pox, is a rare but debilitating illness
that affects Shadowhunters and is caused by inappropriate
contact with demons. The illness is not often seen, because
this kind of inappropriate contact is, luckily, not common.
Mundanes are immune to the disease; it is assumed to be
caused by the interaction of demon poisons with the angelic
nature of Shadowhunters.

The first signs of demon pox are a shield-shaped rash on
the back of the sufferer, which then spreads over the body,
creating fissures in the skin. From this point the afflicted
Shadowhunter will deteriorate physically, experiencing
fever, chills, nausea, oozing sores, non-oozing sores,
buboes, a film of black over the eyes, hair ejection, and
other similar signs of distress. In time the sores and fissures
cover the skin of the victim entirely, and they form a dark
chrysalis within which the victim transforms, painfully
and over the course of several weeks, into a demon himself.
Once the demon emerges from the chrysalis, the previously
existing person is in effect deceased, and the only end to the
torment is to kill the demon.

In earlier times astriola was invariably lethal, and not
much could be done for the sufferer but to make him
comfortable and to remove him from innocents who
might be harmed when his full demonic alteration took
place. The progress of the disease could be slowed but not
stopped, and in many cases the victim would choose not
to be treated, since by and large treatment would only
prolong his agony. Today there exist reliable cures that can
clear up demon pox in its early stages, and the illness now
causes few fatalities. It can, however, still be incurable if the
sufferer reaches a certain stage of demonification before

being treated. In addition, a fairly serious stigma is still associated with the disease, and its presence is considered sufficient evidence for the violation of the Law against consorting with demons. Thus those who are treated for demon pox today often receive this treatment while in the prisons of the Silent City.

DISCUSSION QUESTIONS AND THINGS TO TRY

1. Try: Learning a few words of Purgatic or Cthonic!
   Your local Institute should contain copies of several
   phrase books.

   I recommend the classic Learn Purgatic in Ten to Twelve Years of Misery.
   Do you plan to order lunch in a lot of demon restaurants? No. Is it worth it?
   Then no. The demons who are smart enough to have a conversation usually speak a human language.

2. For those of you with the Sight, have you ever seen a
   demon prior to your time among the Shadowhunters?
   If so, how did your mind process what you were seeing?

   Insert joke about Mrs. Thomson from seventh grade here. WELL, THERE WAS MRS. THOMSON—

   OH, YOU RUINED IT, NEVER MIND.

3. Demons are fond of promising their victims that
   which their heart most desires. What are some things
   a demon might promise you, and how might it manage
   to fulfill those desires in an ironically horrific way?
   It is worth considering these so that if a demon actually
   offers you what your heart most desires, you will not
   be taken in by its lies.

   A demon might promise me a pony.
   He might manage to fulfill those desires in a horrible
   way by giving me a plastic toy pony, or a really
   angry pony that attacks people, or a pony covered in
   sharp spikes so that you can't ride him.

   Your homework: Figure out how to take
   these discussion questions more seriously!

CHAPTER FOUR

Bestiaire Part II:
DOWNWORLDERS

If demons marauding across our world were the only creatures that had to be kept in check by Shadowhunters, our lives would be notably easier. Demons, except for the rare shape-shifting varieties, are usually obviously inhuman, and they are conveniently universally malevolent. In the relations between humans and demons there are no politics, no negotiations. There is just war. They attack; we defend.

But the whole of the world is not that simple. Once demons began to trespass into the lives of humans, the waters of good and evil became muddied, and the muddied waters of humanity became Downworlders. Some Downworlders—warlocks and the fey—predate the Nephilim by untold years. But the youngest Downworlders, werewolves and vampires, are a relatively recent phenomenon, the result of demon diseases previously unknown that have crept into the human race and, it seems, are with us for good.

—— WEREWOLVES ——

There wolves! Are you going to do this in every chapter?

The earlier of these demon diseases is lycanthropy, which is *Maybe!* believed to have first appeared in the forests of Central Europe sometime in (probably) the thirteenth century. Lycanthropy is believed to have spread rapidly through Europe and then more slowly to the rest of the world. Persecuting and publicly burning werewolves was in vogue late in the fifteenth century and early in the sixteenth century, which corresponded to a similar fashion for burning so-called witches (almost never actually Downworlders; see "The Hunts and the Schism," in Appendix A).

Lycanthropy transforms a human into a werewolf, a demi-human whose demonic infection causes them to transform into a large and dangerous wolf under the light of the full moon. Worse, werewolves in their lupine form are not merely wolves. They possess unnatural—demonic—strength and speed, and their claws and fangs are able to slash through a chain-link fence or bite through a padlock. Without help and training a werewolf can be a very dangerous creature. When lycanthropy is at its worst, a man lives what appears to be a normal mundane existence, only to become a vicious, uncontrolled, murdering beast roughly three nights each month, retaining no memory of his own evil acts.

IF YOU MEET A WEREWOLF

A werewolf who is in his or her usual human form, and not under the influence of the lycanthropic Change, is no different from any other human. You should approach any new werewolves in human form as you would anybody else. Contrary to common belief, they will not smell you or challenge you to mortal combat.

If you encounter a werewolf in wolf form, you must quickly assess the situation. If he is ignoring you, move away from the area calmly but quickly. If he is watching you, look for the signs of aggression you would look for in a dog—bared teeth, growling, hackles raised. Raise your hands to show you are not a threat. *Also try to love*

Defend yourself only if attacked, and try to incapacitate the wolf, not kill him. A werewolf who is attacking a human is almost always responding out of terror, or is newly made and not yet in control of himself.

If you know the werewolf in question, *do not* attempt to reason with him by calling him by his human name or reminding him of all of the fun human things you have done together. Also *do not* try to give him commands like you would a dog (such as "heel" or "stay").

as little bite a roast beef as possible

WHERE DID WEREWOLVES ORIGINALLY COME FROM? HOW DO THEY LIVE?

It is not known what demon, or demon species, is responsible for the first appearance of werewolves. There is a conjectured Greater Demon of origin, who is usually referred to by the placeholder name "Wolf" in literature. Despite many supposed descriptions of Wolf in medieval writing, there exists no credible candidate for who he might be. He seems to have appeared, created werewolves, and left our world forever.

New werewolves are created when a human is bitten by an existing werewolf. Approximately half the time a werewolf bite will cause lycanthropy in the victim. Many safeguards against bites are now in place, and much organizational work has been done by the Nephilim and by werewolves themselves (see the sidebar on the Praetor Lupus, page 87) to prevent unexpected attacks, which means that rogue werewolf bites are happily a rare occurrence today.

The job of the newmade werewolf, his new responsibility, is to gain control of his transformation, or "Change." Control in this area is more important than any other adjustment he makes to his new life. Werewolves can in fact live peaceful and calm lives among mundanes, more so than other Downworlders, with proper training and self-possession. By the regulation of the Praetor Lupus, any werewolf who cannot consciously control his or her Changing is deemed a rogue, whatever his or her other behavior. This regulation is intended to motivate werewolves to learn to control their Change—in order to get the Praetor off their backs; an accidental attack is a disaster for the Praetor and the werewolf community, and they require strong rules to prevent such a thing.

This is particularly important because newly made were-wolves do not normally transition gently into their new lives. Along with the lycanthropic response often comes uncontrolled aggression and rage, suicidal anger, and depression. This raft of emotions is both terrible and potentially dangerous in the hands of a newly strengthened and powered Downworlder who no longer knows his own strength. Thus, newly made werewolves must be treated with caution. The Praetor Lupus has taken responsibility for self-policing the Downworlder community of both fledgling vampires (see "Vampires," page 88) and newmade werewolves, and can be of assistance in particularly difficult cases.

By all reports the first Change is the worst because it is a new experience, but let us be clear that the lyncanthropic Change is always a trauma. The stretching and reshaping of muscles and bones is very painful, especially the realignment of the spine. Human teeth are pushed out of the way by wolf fangs painfully tearing from the gums. This and the brain chemistry changes cause most werewolves to go into a fugue during their first Change, and they lose all memory of what they have done as wolves. This is when lycanthropes are at their most dangerous—when they do not yet have control of their Change and cannot yet retain their human mind when Changed.

Worse, most newmade lycanthropes do not yet have a pack affiliation and thus don't have access to information that would help them understand their Change. This is why we recommend mercy to new werewolves even though rogue Downworlders are technically not protected by the Accords. Newmade werewolves are literally not in control of their own faculties. The Praetor Lupus helps enormously in finding and rehabilitating these rogues, and a captured rogue werewolf should usually be brought to a local Praetor office or representative rather than to the nearest pack.

The Praetor has been very successful in their mission and

85

has made werewolves the model Downworlders of self-policing; in most parts of the world, it's rare that Shadowhunters need to be called in to deal with a rogue werewolf, a massive change since the creation of the Praetor. However, even the most controlled werewolf will still be forced into a Change by the full moon, if only on the exact night of the fullest moon. There is, therefore, no such thing as a perfectly safe werewolf.

Moreover, there is no such thing as a safe werewolf pack. There is an inherent violence at the center of traditional werewolf organization: A pack leader can be challenged to mortal combat by any member of the pack, at any time, for leadership of the pack. Apart from making the entire social structure of werewolves centered around ritual killing (an unfortunately common thread in Downworlder cultures), this also means that the werewolf population is constantly committing what mundane society would label as murder in the first degree, and such behavior may attract the attention of mundane law enforcement. Here we may find ourselves needed to perform some glamours and protections to keep the Downworlder and mundane populations away from each other.

An experienced werewolf, one in whom the Change is a well-known companion rather than an unwanted invader, can often learn more advanced shape-shifting—for instance, Changing only one hand into a wolf's paw to cut something with its claws.

Traditionally werewolves and vampires maintain an intense hatred for one another, which is believed to be inherent in their respective demonic infections, but there are places in the world where the two groups get along and are even allies, such as Prague.

Werewolves are mortal and will age and die like any other humans. They are also able to bear children, to whom they *do not* pass on lycanthropy. They can have offspring with a Shadow-hunter as the other parent, and since Shadowhunter blood always

86

breeds true, the child of a werewolf and a Shadowhunter, however rare, will be a Shadowhunter.

WEAKNESSES

In addition to their supernatural strength, grace, and reflexes, werewolves have the same unnaturally accelerated healing abilities as most other Downworlders. They cannot regenerate— if you cut the arm off a werewolf, he will not grow back a new arm—but they can recover from most mundane wounds. The only ways to permanently wound or kill a werewolf are either with the angelic fire of the seraph blade or, more famously, with pure silver. Silver is associated with the moon, and wounds made with silver weapons will cause werewolves not only permanent damage but also great pain. Any Institute will be found to have a cache of silver weapons in place for just this reason.

Showed this section to Luke, and he yelled and paced around for half an hour. I took notes.

THE PRAETOR LUPUS

The Praetor Lupus is the first and largest self-policing organization of the Downworlders. It has grown from a tiny force begun in London in the late nineteenth century to a worldwide organization. The name suggests an old, even ancient, organization, but in fact the Praetor Lupus—"Wolf Guard"—was founded only 150 years ago, and its name is not ancient, but rather reflects the Victorian vogue for all things classical. The founder, Woolsey Scott, was a wealthy werewolf of London and began the Praetor in response to his brother's dying wishes. The self-declared mission of the Praetor is to track down "orphaned" Downworlders—newly made werewolves, fledgling vampires, and warlocks who have no knowledge of their people—and to help them take

It's your diligence as a student that astounds me, really. Also, definitely get Simon a satin cape. You know he wants one.

Apparently overstates the danger of single rogue werewolves. Codex acts like they are like shark in Jaws: just efficient killing machines. Most rogue werewolves in cities are shot by cops; most rogue werewolves in woods on farms starve, die in fights with bears, etc.

• Praetor originally about saving werewolves from being killed by their condition, not saving mundanes from effects of werewolves. • The "model Downworlder" status that Codex condescendingly suggests is actually really offensive. • L. will show them where they can put their model Downworlder status. • This is why the Clave blah, blah, blah Council blah, blah, blah uphill both ways in the snow. • Possible Hanukkah gifts for Simon: new Teyuka box set? silly winter hat? black satin cape? blood?

87

control of their powers and become connected with a clan or pack or mentor warlock.

The Clave and the Praetor have an uneasy relationship, despite their many goals in common. The Praetor prefers to operate without supervision and is very secretive about their methods and their membership; this secrecy makes the Clave uneasy, since Shadowhunters are meant to be the chief protectors of Downworld and we believe in openness and disclosure whenever possible. The Praetor argues, for their part, that their goal is to save rogue Downworlders *before* they have run afoul of Covenant Law, and that close oversight by the Clave would damage their ability to protect their charges. Despite the Accords, over the years the Praetor has become more secretive as it has grown.

The symbol of the Praetor Lupus is easily recognized, and is worn with much pride by its members. The symbol is an imprint of a wolf's paw adorned with the slogan *Beati Bellicosi*, "Blessed Are the Warriors."

—— VAMPIRES ——

DO NOT SKIP. Simon is not a textbook-level source on vampires!

Vampires are victims of another demonic infection, which turns them into drinkers of blood. They possess retractable razorlike fangs that are deployed when their bloodlust is roused. These they sink into a surface vein of their victim, and then the vampire consumes that victim's blood to his or her satisfaction. The act of drinking blood brings a rush of energy and vitality to the vampire. Experienced vampires can resist this rush and cease their drinking in order to leave their victims alive and able to recover, but new

88

Showed this page to Luke. He turned purplish and told me to show it to Jordan. Notes from talking to Jordan: Praetor not actually that secretive. Secretive from Clave specifically. What Clave calls secrecy, Praetor calls not telling Clave every single thing about themselves and their operations. Claim of Clave's love of openness obviously some kind of joke. Don't need werewolves to teach me that.

DO NOT SKIP. You must only stroll, mosey, or hop.

vampires may have trouble controlling their urge to drink their victims to the point of death. Worse, after the initial sting of a vampire bite, the poison contained within vampire saliva dulls the victim's pain and may make the experience pleasurable for the victim. The poison acts as a muscle relaxant and a euphoric, and even a strong Shadowhunter will respond to its effects. A well-Marked Shadowhunter can, of course, retain her consciousness much longer than a mundane, but there is still a heavy risk associated with being bitten.

Unlike werewolves, vampires are considered to be "undead"; that is, their bodies are no longer alive in the sense that ours are. Their human souls reside in animated corpses, kept intact and animate by the demon disease. They cannot bear children and can create new vampires only by their infecting bite.

IF YOU MEET A VAMPIRE

Do not look the vampire directly in the eyes. Do not expose your neck or the insides of your wrists to the vampire. Do not go with a vampire you don't know to a second location strange to you. Do not drink from a goblet given to you by the vampire, no matter how much they insist it is safe. There is no need to be deferential, but they do not take insults lightly. Do not mock the vampire's hair or clothes. They place an enormous weight on whether they are being treated respectfully, and while under the Law they may not harm us, it is usually wise to avoid earning the enmity of a vampire.

Do not taunt the vampire. Do not tell him his T-shirt is stupid. Do not call him "the Vampman" or "Dr. Teeth" or anything like that.

Aw, Fangs over there makes a good point.

WHERE DO VAMPIRES COME FROM?

When two vampires love each other very much . . .

Vampirism is the other great result of demon infection in humans, and vampires have a well-established pedigree, as befits a people obsessed with ritual and protocol. Unlike in the case of lycanthropy, we know exactly the who, the when, and the where of the first vampires. They were created in a public ceremony for which the Nephilim have multiple written accounts, from those who claim to have been present. The Greater Demon Hecate, sometimes (and confusingly) called "the Mother of Witches," was summoned in a massive blood-based sacrifice held in 1444 at the Court of Wallachia, in what is now Romania. The then-ruler of Wallachia, Vlad III, had a great circle of prisoners of war impaled on tall wooden spikes, and in exchange for this impressive sacrifice Hecate transformed Vlad and the large majority of his court into the first vampires. *Vampire origin, surprisingly metal.*

Vampirism did not spread seriously as a disease until a few years later, when Vlad led a series of raids into neighboring Transylvania. There he and his men appear to have gorged themselves on their enemies and spread vampirism through the entire region. The city of Cluj became the site of the first vampire clan officially recognized by the Clave, and Transylvania took over as the epicenter of the vampire epidemic. For whatever reason, Vlad and his men did not create any significant number of vampires in their own home area, and vampire activity in Wallachia diminished to near silence after Vlad's death.

In a stroke of historiographical luck, the Cluj Institute in the late fifteenth century was home to a Shadowhunter named Simion. We know almost nothing about him, not even his family name—he only ever refers to himself as "Simion the Scribe"—but he provided a clear and detailed picture of the original spread of the vampire plague. He describes what can only be called an

90

In 1444 in Wallachia, THE VAMPIRES ALL CAME FORTH TO ROCK US, MM

Just no.

all-out war between the Nephilim and the earliest vampire clans, with mundanes taken from their beds and left drained in the street, vampires chained to the ground in village squares and left to burn alive in the sun, and other such horrors. Shadowhunters, especially those already experienced at hunting Downworlders, traveled to Transylvania for the sole purpose of vampire slaying; new vampires continued to appear just as fast as old ones could be killed. Within months the Cluj Institute, formerly one of the smallest and least important Institutes in Europe, had become the epicenter for the largest demonic epidemic the mundane world had ever seen. Chaos arose, as neither Nephilim nor vampires yet understood how new vampires were made or how they could be reliably killed. *I AM ACTUALLY NOT FINDING THIS SECTION TO BE THE LIGHTHEARTED FUN I HAD HOPED.* Reading about people like you being killed will do that.

The war ended with no clear winner. Knowledge of the vampiric disease grew, vampirism spread to other parts of Europe, and Shadowhunters returned home to sign treaties with local vampire clans and keep the peace in their own territories. Transylvania remained a devastated battleground for hundreds of years, where mortality rates for both vampires and Shadowhunters remained the highest in the world, and where the authority of the Clave was tenuous at best. Only with the unofficial end of the Schism in the first half of the eighteenth century did the battle die down, and today the Cluj Institute is, while more vampire-focused than most other Institutes, no busier or more dangerous than any other, and Shadowhunters visit not to wage war but to see the Muzeul de Vampiri, where magically animated wax figures re-create the carnage of five hundred years ago.

Exposure, the practice of binding vampires outside to be burned alive by the rising sun, was banned in the Third Accords of 1902 after the popularity of Bram Stoker's 1897 novel *Dracula* led to an enthusiasm for hunting and brutally killing innocent, Law-abiding vampires.

WHAT ARE VAMPIRES LIKE?

There is as much variation in vampires as there is in humans, of course, but generally speaking, vampires tend to be pale, sallow, and thin, as though weakened by malnourishment or some wasting disease. Contrary to this appearance, like werewolves they possess superhuman strength, grace, and speed. Also contrary to this semblance of death, their blood shimmers a bright red, much brighter than the blood of humans. Also like werewolves, vampires heal quickly from mundane injuries.

Vampires more than other Downworlders seem to have one foot in Hell already and to not be entirely present in our world. This is believed to be the reason why vampires cast no reflections in mirrors and do not leave footprints or fingerprints as they move through the world. They cannot be tracked by normal tracking magic, either demonic or Nephilimic. (Powerful vampires, however, tend to travel with mundane subjugates who can be tracked.) Vampires are comfortable in darkness; their eyes adjust to seeing in darkness and seeing in light almost instantly, much faster than the eyes of humans.

The dirt of the grave in which a vampire was buried holds special properties for that vampire. She can tell, for instance, if that grave has been disturbed, or is being trod upon, or if dirt from that grave is removed from its site. Vampires have cleverly made use of this power to communicate simple messages over long distances—for instance, breaking a container of a vampire's grave dirt could be used to alert and summon that vampire. *SHOULDA SAVED SOME OF THAT DIRT . . .*

The final vampire power worthy of mention here is perhaps the most dangerous: the *encanto*, or "fascination." Vampires can, with simple prolonged eye contact, convince mundanes and even Shadowhunters of almost anything, and can persuade them into almost any act. This is a skill that must be developed and practiced by vampires, and so it is typically the older and more powerful vampires that make use of it. If you live in an area particularly rife with vampire activity, you should consult your local Institute about prioritizing training to resist the *encanto*.

MY FIRST ALBUM WILL BE TITLED ONE FOOT IN HELL ALREADY.

I hereby deem that title "Totally Stupid."

VAMPIRES AND THE LAW

You love THAT TITLE! You CANNOT RESIST THE ENCANTO!

Many new Shadowhunters are surprised to learn that it is not against the Law for a vampire to drink blood from a human, provided that the human remains alive. This is because of the healing properties of vampire saliva. When a vampire drinks from a victim, it increases the red blood cell count in that victim, making them stronger, healthier, and able to live longer. The effect is small, but it mitigates the weakening effect of losing blood, and so a bitten human usually remains unharmed.

93

Nevertheless, the risk of accidentally killing a human by drinking from him too deeply, and the general sense of menace around having one's blood drained, have led most "civilized" vampires to eschew drinking from living human victims (other than subjugates; see page 98) in favor of pre-drawn blood or the blood of animals. By the Accords, vampires must abide by the same mundane laws against murder as any other Downworlders, but vampires are the only Downworlders who might commit murder for food, potentially for survival. It is notable, and admirable, that so many vampires have voluntarily committed themselves to the same respect for human life as the other signers of the Accords.

Now Simon is angry too. He and Luke are both pacing around yelling at nobody about the Codex. Summary: "Only vampires murder for food? That is rich." It's hard being the Monster Manual.

VAMPIRE POLITICS

Like werewolves, vampires consider themselves to be on some level brethren with all other vampires, no matter what clan they are affiliated with. A vampire who raised a hand against another, except in the rare circumstance of a clan war, would be considered anathema by the vampire community, and his life would be forfeit. The Nephilim generally stay out of these matters of internal justice, although we will sometimes intervene to arbitrate conflicts between clans to stave off full-out battle. When clan wars do occur, leadership changes, as it does with werewolves: Whoever kills the head of a vampire clan becomes its leader.

Among Downworlders only faeries are more committed to notions of honor and etiquette than vampires. Vampires are often found making oaths and vows, which they take very seriously. These vows are usually written and signed in blood—not a surprise, given the vampire obsession with blood generally. These blood-oaths are binding: Vampires are compelled by the oaths' contents and cannot violate them unless the bond is broken through further, and more onerous, ritual. A vampire who has thus sworn an oath to you under these circumstances can be trusted to follow at least the letter of the oath in the strictest detail. Conversely, you should be suspicious of a vampire who is willing to make a promise to you but will not swear to that promise in blood.

I wish Simon would vow to return my Ghibli DVDs. | *I so vow!* *In bloooooood?* | Never mind!

WEAKNESSES

Obviously it would be the preference of all Nephilim to never be forced to bring harm to a vampire, but history teaches us that it is wise to know how to defend oneself against them, and what their strengths and weaknesses might entail. The Accords require that vampires turn away from their natures as hunters and predators, just as humans must choose to turn away from our own abilities to kill and harm.

Vampires are extremely vulnerable to fire. While they are much stronger and more durable in many ways than mundanes and Nephilim, their bodies are weaker and less resistant to burning than humans'. They are likely, when exposed to fire, to burst into flames in the manner of paper, dry wood, or similarly flammable objects. As such, vampires not only can be harmed by fire but can often be kept at bay by a protective boundary of fire or a burning torch.

Holy water, and other common blessed materials, such as angelically aligned swords, are harmful to vampires and will scorch and burn their flesh.

More generally, holy symbols may be anathema to vampires if the symbols hold weight with the specific vampire addressed. A crucifix may repel a vampire who held Christian beliefs before he was Turned, but a vampire who was raised as a person in a Buddhist faith would not generally respond. In the early days of vampire

95

hunting, when there was much less migration of peoples away from their home cultures, holy symbols were more dependable as vampire repellent, but in our modern age of religious pluralism and because of the ease with which people can move around the world, it has become unwise to depend on this method.

Along similar lines, older guidebooks to the Shadow World suggest that a vampire trying to hide his demonic nature can be sussed out by his inability to speak the name of God. This is also no longer reliably true. Most vampires that as mortals did not ascribe to a religious faith do not develop an aversion to holy names as part of their Turning. In addition, older and more powerful vampires often regain the ability to speak holy names, although it's not clear whether this is because the aversion fades over time or because as the vampires age, they descend more deeply into the demonic and become able to speak God's name as a curse.

As mentioned before, vampires cannot stand the direct light of the sun. Mythology tells us that this is a facet of their status as demonic, damned creatures, that they are cursed to not be able to look at the sun that gives life to Earth. Whatever the reason, sunlight burns the skin of vampires, as does (to a lesser extent) witchlight, being light of angelic origin. Artificial light, such as that of gaslight and electric light, may cause discomfort in vampires if it is strong enough, but they are normally able to remain undamaged unless already very weak. *Also, fluorescent light is avoided, as it's unflattering.*

A ray of sunlight will cause burns on a vampire's skin, but full exposure to the sun—being exposed fully to unblocked sunshine—will cause them to burst into flame dramatically, and they will be consumed and put to rest quickly. For this reason vampires are normally careful to remain dormant and inactive during daylight hours. *Unless he is a SUPERVAMPIRE, of course.*

TREATING VAMPIRE BITES   Important! Note! Why's it gotta be like that, man?

If a vampire bites and drinks blood from a victim,
no supernatural treatment may be needed. Normal
Shadowhunter wound-care protocols apply—the use
of an *iratze* or other healing Marks, and treatment for
blood loss and shock if the draining has been severe.
Mundanes also can have their blood taken by vampires
with no permanent ill effects, provided the wounds are
cared for and not too much blood has been taken.

The real danger lies in the case of a human who has
consumed vampire blood. Even if not enough blood is
consumed to cause the death and rebirth of the victim as a
vampire, the smallest amount of vampire blood is enough
to create in the victim an irresistible pull to vampires,
which could cause that victim to become a subjugate,
begging to be Turned.

The proper treatment for the consumption of vampire
blood is emetic: The victim must be made to drink holy
water until all of the vampire blood is out of his system.
The victim is likely to be very sick during this process—he
will of course cough up everything in his system, not just
the vampire blood, and the presence of the blood is likely to
have made him fevered and hot to the touch. This process
is, however, much better than the alternative.

Even a small amount of vampire blood consumed may
require the consumption of quite a lot of holy water. This
is a case where it is better to be safe and consume too much
holy water than too little. The victim can be assumed to be
healthy and cured when the consumption of holy water no
longer produces the emetic response.

SUBJUGATES

Powerful vampires will often decide that, rather than feeding haphazardly on whatever blood they can find, they would prefer a ready supply. They will then create a vampire subjugate: They will select a victim and keep him close by, drinking from him and also feeding him small amounts of vampire blood. This vampire blood will make the subjugate docile, obedient, and, in time, worshipful of his vampire master. The subjugate will cease eating food and will survive entirely on a mix of animal blood and vampire blood. He will not become a full vampire, but subjugates are kept in a suspended animation, their aging process drastically slowed (although they are not immortal and will eventually die).

A subjugate who is turned into a vampire loses his obedient and worshipful nature and becomes a normal vampire, like any other.

Most subjugates are young in appearance; vampires revere youth and beauty and tend to prefer their subjugates to possess both. (A practical consideration is also present. The younger the subjugate, the less chance that he will turn out to have diseased or otherwise problematic blood.)

Subjugates are sometimes known as darklings. Although the term is archaic, it is still used in some formal vampire rituals today. Vampires love nothing so much as formal rituals.

The culture of subjugates among vampires is that, first, they are no longer human but are something else, and therefore are not afforded the rights and respect granted to humans. Subjugation is in essence voluntary slavery; subjugates effectively consent to become the property of their vampire masters, renounce their human names, and so on. A subjugate would never introduce himself to another vampire or another subjugate, for instance; it would be his master's choice whether to communicate his name, or indeed, whether the subjugate would possess an identifying name at all.

The creation of new subjugates was made illegal in the Seventh Accords of 1962. Vampires who had subjugates created prior to the Accords were allowed to keep them. The Law also continues to allow vampires to transfer existing subjugates to other vampires. These two facts have made it almost impossible to convict vampires for creating subjugates. Vampires simply claim that their subjugates predate the Accords, and since the subjugates' identities and lives are tracked by the vampires themselves, it is very hard to prove otherwise.

FLEDGLINGS

NOTE: DID NOT READ. TOO SOON.

A human who has consumed enough vampire blood to be themselves transformed into a vampire does not, as some popular mundane stories would have it, abruptly turn from a living human in one moment to a vampire in the next. The human—who is known in vampire culture as a "fledgling"—must die, be buried, and, in being reborn, make his way out of his grave of his own power. (In the rare and sad case that a Shadowhunter is irreversibly turned into a vampire, this is the one circumstance in which her body may be buried rather than burned.)

Like a ghost, a fledgling rising from his grave draws energy and strength from the living things nearby, drawing their heat and producing a distinctive cold spot around his grave. When he has risen, he will be nearly feral and starving for the blood that will, for eternity, sustain him. This is why fledglings are the most dangerous of vampires. Sometimes a vampire clan will turn a human to a vampire purposefully, and in those cases the transition usually goes smoothly. The clan can be present for the vampire's rising, can make sure he is able to successfully rise, and can supply him with blood and take him to a safe place to recover.

99

This is, however, not the way that most vampires are made; most are made by accident. In those cases the fledgling is buried by his friends and family, as any other mundane would be, and rises unexpectedly, in a mundane location, desperate for blood and barely knowing himself. These are the circumstances that lead to vampire attacks and the deaths of mundanes. While such an out-of-control fledgling must be stopped, it is not the policy of the Shadowhunters to consider these fledglings rogue vampires, and thus the fledglings should be turned over either to a local vampire clan or, preferably, to the Praetor Lupus, both of which are well-equipped to take care of the fledgling's needs.

WARLOCKS

Perhaps no other Downworlders have a more complex relationship with Shadowhunters than do warlocks. The off-spring of demons and mundanes, warlocks do not have the many unifying features of werewolves or vampires, or even of faeries. The only things that can be said to be true of all warlocks are that (1) they possess a so-called warlock mark on their body that identifies them as not merely human, (2) like most hybrid species they are sterile, and (3) they possess the ability to perform magic. It is this last feature that makes them at once the most powerful of Downworlders and the most closely tied to Shadowhunters. For the whole of our history we have worked in concert with warlocks, whether as partners or (more commonly) as hired specialists, to allow us to make use of some of the demonic magic that our own powers exclude us from.

Needless to say, warlocks are rarely born from an affectionate relationship between a demon and a human. Instead they are

created through one of the two worst depredations demons visit upon our world. Most obviously, there are warlocks born from demons violating humans against their will. This was the predominant means of warlock conception in the time before the Incursion, when demons were rare and normally appeared in isolation. Today, though, demons are much less likely to manifest themselves openly, since the presence of Shadowhunters and the much larger number of Downworlders makes them more likely to be discovered and attacked. Therefore, today most warlocks are the result of a different kind of violation: the coupling of a human with an Eidolon demon (see "Demonologie," Chapter 3) who is disguised as the human's loved one.

Warlocks cannot be produced from the union of a demon and a Shadowhunter; because the angelic Shadowhunter blood and the demonic blood both normally dominate, the combination cannot create a living child. The offspring of a Shadowhunter and a demon is death.

IF YOU MEET A WARLOCK

Nothing can be generally said to be true of meetings with warlocks; these Downworlders vary in temperament and quality as much as humans as a whole. It is only noted here that it is considered impolite to stare at a warlock's mark (see page 104).

WARLOCKS AND MAGIC

All warlocks are to some extent practitioners of magic. Some inherit more magical aptitude than others, and those who cultivate that aptitude may become quite powerful among warlocks and quite useful to the Nephilim. The most gifted may find themselves able to study demonic magic in the secretive Spiral Labyrinth, the central home of warlock magical research and knowledge. Unlike Nephilim, warlocks do inherently possess magic. They have invented quite a lot of new magic, in fact, which is dutifully recorded and kept in the Labyrinth. The location of the Labyrinth is unknown even to the Nephilim, and possibly it exists in its own pocket dimension separate from our world. Its age is also unknown. According to our earliest Nephilimic writings, it was already considered ancient in the time of Elphas the Unsteady (see Excerpts from A *History of the Nephilim*, Appendix A). The magic by which one may travel there is one of the most closely guarded secrets in all the world, and it's whispered that a *geas* placed on all warlocks at the moment of their birth guarantees that if a warlock reveals the Labyrinth's location to a non-warlock, the result would be instant and blindingly painful death.   It is also whispered that this is completely bogus.

The warlocks have in some ways suffered more than any other Downworlders; they have neither the clan communities of werewolves and vampires nor the sacred home of the fey, and have had to make their way in our world largely by their own individual courage and cunning. The Nephilim have not always provided a safe haven for warlocks—for example, turning on them and slaughtering them by the hundreds in the time of the Schism (see Appendix A). Today we can only mourn the loss of trust and cooperation that once existed between warlocks and Shadowhunters. Relations between the two have improved greatly since the Accords, which guarantee not only the rights of warlocks but legal permission for them to perform demonic magic when acting to assist a Nephilim investigation. It is likely, though, that the kind of mutual assistance, angelic and demonic together in the form of Nephilim and warlocks, that marked the great flourishing of magic in the Middle Ages will never again be seen. *Too bad about all that slaughtering, Clave. Not exactly making me swell with pride about my people here.*

WARLOCK MARKS

Every warlock has some feature on his body that labels him as not fully human. These marks (not to be confused with the Marks of Raziel that we use) are as varied as demonkind and range from the subtle to the glaringly obvious. A warlock's fate among the mundanes may well be decided not by himself or by his origins but by whether he is marked with, for example, strangely colored eyes or unusual height, or with blue skin or ram's horns or tiger stripes or a shiny black carapace. Any unusual feature can of course be glamoured into invisibility, but the warlock mark is present from birth, and recall that most mundanes are unaware of anything strange about their child until he is born and his mark is revealed. Even among those parents fully aware of the partially demonic parentage of their child, a warlock mark may be a deeply unpleasant surprise. These marks seem unrelated to the particular type of demon parent; it is not so much the inheritance of a demonic feature as the arbitrary mutation of the body in response to demonic magic coursing through it. *Note: Magnus's eyes.*

Hey baby, guess where my warlock mark is.

IFRITS
Never works. Trust me. Never works.

Rarely, but sometimes, a warlock is born who, though the child of a demon and a human, has no access to demonic magic. These unfortunate souls have the disadvantages of a warlock—the warlock aspect that marks them as not fully human—but cannot perform magic. These so-called ifrits are trapped on the limens of the magical world, suffering the stigma of their inhuman marks without the benefit of supernatural power. Historically they have fallen into the underclass of the supernatural world, and are often found working on the wrong side of the Law, unable to live in the mundane world but unable to find a respectable life in the Shadow World.

Sometimes, of course, an ifrit is born with a warlock mark that can be easily hidden from public view. These "ghost ifrits" can sometimes make their way through mundane human society without complication, and as such may have no doings with the Shadow World at all. Today most ifrits with marks that are difficult to disguise acquire magical artifacts that provide them with a permanent glamour and live away from the magical world, unable to have children of their own but otherwise unremarkable to mundanes.

—— FAERIES ——

NOTE: THE FAIR FOLK ARE NOT ACTUALLY FAIR. THEY ARE BIG CHEATERS IN FACT.

Strange they may be, alien to us, more unknown than demons themselves, but the fey, the faeries, are Downworlders. They are people—they have souls. They are the least understood of all magical peoples, the great ancient mystery of our world. They are found in countless varieties, sizes, and types, and in all environments.

Most properly these creatures are known as "faeries," after their homeland, the realm of Faerie. They are known in literature by many other names, partly because of their enormous variety and partly because of age-old superstitions about invoking them by name. Most commonly they are called the fey, but you will also hear them named the Fair Folk, or the Kind Ones, or the Little People, or any number of other euphemisms.

UNICORN		SEELIE KNIGHT	SEELIE QUEEN	PIXIE	BROWNIES	

IF YOU MEET A FAERIE

Do not sign any contracts or agree to any bargains with faeries. Faeries love to haggle but will usually do so only if they are sure they will win. Do not eat or drink anything a faerie gives you. Do not go attend their magical revels under the hills. They will paint a beautiful picture of what awaits you there, but its beauty is false and hollow. Do not tease a faerie about their height. Do not expect direct answers to direct questions. Do expect indirect answers to indirect questions.

Faeries will always exactly follow the letter of any promise they have made, but expect results delivered with great irony.

Many Shadowhunters have been taken in, despite these rules, by a belief that the particular faerie they met was simpleminded, naive, generous, and so on. This playacting is yet another ploy.

This is a little harsh. Faeries not that bad.

I don't think I agree!

WHERE DO FAERIES COME FROM?

The fey are originally the offspring of demons and angels, with the beauty of angels and the viciousness of demons. (Obviously, since angels are rarely if ever seen in our world in current times, the vast majority of faeries are the offspring of other faeries, just as most Shadowhunters are the offspring of other Shadowhunters and not born from the Cup.) The Fair Folk cannot be said to be morally aligned with either of their parent races. They are good and evil tangled up, following neither the morality of Heaven nor the immorality of Hell but rather their own capricious code of behavior. They are known for their cunning and their cruel sense of humor, and they delight especially in tricking humans—mundanes and Shadowhunters alike. They frequently seek to bargain with humans, offering someone his heart's desire but failing to mention that that desire comes with a terrible cost. They are very long-lived and become only more artful and powerful as they age.

They are the other Downworlders, along with werewolves, who can bear children. They can also have offspring with humans. These offspring will be human and not fey, but they often retain some faerielike aspects or have a penchant for certain kinds of fey magic. It's widely believed, for instance, that humans who naturally possess the Sight have inherited it from some faerie ancestor.

As with werewolves, the children of faeries and Shadow-hunters will be Shadowhunters.

Although the fey are active members of Downworld, and signers of the Accords, faeries are more removed from the affairs of our world than any other known creatures except angels. They usually keep to themselves, and have their own complex politics and social structures, which only tangentially affect our world.

| OGRE | UNSEELIE QUEEN | UNSEELIE KNIGHT | KNOCKER | GOBLIN |

Commonly they are organized into courts, with sovereigns presiding over specific territories in our world and in theirs. However, there are just as many, if not more, free-ranging faeries in the world unaffiliated with any specific monarch. Just as the fey delight in manipulating humans, they delight in manipulating one another, and usually if the problems of the fey intrude into our world, it is the result of conflicts between rival courts, sometimes playful, sometimes serious and brutal.

FEY AND MAGIC

The magic of the fey is, as far as we know, unique in the world. It is very powerful but neither demonically nor seraphically allied, and it cannot be learned or wielded by any creatures other than the fey themselves. This magic is slippery and chaotic and is not easily given to structure and rules that can be learned. Nephilim Marks exist that can protect you from faerie glamours, but you should never, ever allow yourself to feel safe or at ease in the presence of faeries. Believing yourself to have the upper hand in a negotiation with a faerie is a sure sign that you are being deceived and will suffer for it in the end.

Why, then, if they are so removed from our world, do the fey continue to interact with humans as much as they do? The answer lies in genetics.

The biggest problem facing the fey in our modern world is the thinning of their blood. Over time the problem of extensive interbreeding leads to the weakening of family lines. For this reason faeries spend much of their time luring humans into their world. They pursue this in two ways: by creating changelings (see below) and by enticing adult humans into their revels. Much faerie magic exists to trap these reveling humans in Faerie forever, or at least for a long enough time that either they "go native" and forget their former lives or they can be used to produce new faerie children.

There are ways for mundanes (and Shadowhunters) to successfully join the faerie revels without trapping themselves in Faerie. A faerie could be convinced (or bargained with) to give a human a token of safe passage—usually something like a leaf or a flower. And a faerie who voluntarily brings a specific human to the revels can offer his protection and guarantee the human's ability to leave. These bargains, however, are subject to the usual faerie trickery and duplicity, and mundanes and Shadowhunters alike should beware.

CHANGELINGS

The most common contact that the fey have with mundanes is in the making of changelings. It is not dissimilar from the manner whereby the Nephilim create new Shadowhunters with the Mortal Cup, but in the case of the fey, the mundanes gain no benefit. The faeries sneak into a mundane home, take a suitable child, and replace it with a sickly member of their own race. The human child thus grows up in Faerie, able to bring fresh strong blood into the faerie lines, while the mundanes find themselves forced to parent a dying child terrified of iron. It's generally believed that the faeries exchange one of their own partly to allay the suspicions of mundanes and partly out of a twisted, and very fey, sense of fair exchange.

By some method unknown to us, mundane children raised in Faerie take on fey attributes, and can perform some faerie magic. By the same token the fey child left in the mundane world, if he survives, typically never knows his own origin. Apart from a predilection for the Sight, he may never come to know anything of the magical world at all.

By Covenant Law we are forbidden from interfering with this process of child exchange. This ruling has been debated hotly at several of the Accords proceedings over the past hundred years, but both of the children are raised in loving homes—the fey choose the unwitting adoptive parents of their offspring carefully—and no better solution for refreshing the faerie bloodlines has been found. Pragmatism leads Nephilim to prefer that the fey create changelings rather than abduct adult mundanes into their revels.

THE LAND OF FAERIE

The realm of Faerie is not one that is welcoming to Shadowhunters, and in general Nephilim should avoid spending time there.

Despite our powers and our Sight, we are still as susceptible to the lures and dangers of Faerie as most mundanes. The fey have always been clear that their signing of the Accords represents their covenant for behavior in our realm, not in theirs. Faerie is older than the Accords, older than the Nephilim, and it possesses its own magic that the Gray Book can only partly and imperfectly protect against, at best.

That said, Faerie does have rules, and those rules do not leave Nephilim helpless. A Shadowhunter who is the victim of an unprovoked independent attack by a creature of Faerie is allowed by fey law to defend herself. If the attacking creature is killed, the fey are likely to shrug and explain that the creature's decision to attack was his own, and if that decision turned out poorly, it was not the problem of other fey. (One must, of course, be careful that such an attack is not on the orders of some other creature or court; it is always worth remembering that the only thing that the fey like more than meddling in human affairs is their own internal political fights. A Shadowhunter who became a piece in one of the faeries' elaborate games of human chess would be very unlucky indeed.)

Entrances to Faerie tend to be hidden, rather than guarded, and tend to be permanently located in a single place. (The fey may close an entrance and open a new one when the original entrance has become dangerous or unworkable, or in the rare case when wars break out between fey courts and entrances must be closed or guarded.) Faerie entrances are normally found in natural surroundings rather than in man-made areas, and they are often given away by some aspect of their natural appearance that is "wrong" or "off"—a tree in an impossibly specific shape, a reflection in water that does not match the world above the reflection, an apparently empty cave from which faint music can be heard if all else is quiet.

For the most part it is wise for Shadowhunters to avoid Faerie. Though it is described as a realm and one can travel in it like in a country, it does not tolerate being surveyed and does not have a consistent layout. Seasons can change in the blink of an eye, mountains and caverns can appear where minutes before no such things were visible, and its rivers change their courses at the whim of some unknown force. No map of Faerie has ever been produced. Do not wander there; you are likely to join the untold throng of humans who have crossed the borders into the feylands and never returned.

WHAT A SURPRISE, THAT WE ARE ALL MIXED UP WITH FAERIE STUFF THAT WE SHOULD ABSOLUTELY POSITIVELY AVOID. HAVE WE AS A GROUP EVER MET A WARNING WE DIDN'T IGNORE?

Speak for yourself, Fangs.

DISCUSSION QUESTIONS AND THINGS TO TRY

1. What is your favorite Downworlder? Why?

   Warlocks, because they are fabulous!

   OFFENDED. ALSO, MANY WARLOCKS NOT FABULOUS. ONLY THE ONE WE KNOW.

   Vampires, because they keep bothering me. This question is stupid.

2. Do you have any prejudices about any Downworlders
   that might affect your ability to work with them? If so,
   it is important to recognize these biases and discuss
   them with the head of your Institute before you begin
   active service.

   Vampires keep bothering me, a werewolf gives me my curfew, a warlock hid my memories from me, and faeries are just constantly messing with me.

   The part where you've learned that Downworlders are a pain in the neck is accurate.

3. Have you been tested to see if you possess *Honestly, the stuff*
   inherited faerie or werewolf blood? It may affect *Downworlders*
   your ability to take on certain Marks. Symptoms *have done is*
   to look for include naturally occurring Sight *nothing compared to*
   and frequent cravings for red meat, respectively. *what Shadowhunters have done to me,*

   Um, no, actually, I haven't. *so . . .*

   I think you're pretty safe. Both of your parents were full Shadowhunters, and one of them was obsessed with blood purity.

   I bet Valentine had a werewolf grandmother or something. That's usually how that kind of thing turns out.

   I just wrote a thing, but it was not appropriate for a textbook so I erased it.

   A ROOM. YOU TWO. GET ONE.

CHAPTER FIVE

Bestiaire Part III:
ANGELS AND MEN

ANGELS:
OUR MYSTERIOUS PATRONS *also terrifying*

No "If You Meet an Angel" section, Codex? You are not helpful to me at all.

About angels little is known, much is conjectured, and few who might speak knowledgeably live to do so. Of all the supernatural creatures discussed herein, we know the least about angels. They are the great absent generals of our army, having left us a thousand years ago with their heavenly endorsement, basic marching orders, and enough magic to fight for ourselves. Much has been done in their name, both good and evil, even though the number of confirmed manifestations of angels in our world in the entire history of the Nephilim can be counted on one hand.

And yet their blood runs in the veins of every Nephilim, yourself included, flowing into our bodies through the transformative properties of the Mortal Cup. Angels may be absent patrons, but our patrons and spiritual parents they are, and we recognize them with our prayers, our invocations, and in the names of our most holy weapons.

In truth no one knows why angels are so distant from the events of our world. The first great heretical question of Nephilim history is one that has probably already occurred to you: If Raziel and his angels were so determined to wipe the demonic menace from our world, why not do it themselves? Like so many other questions about the nature and purpose of angels, this one remains unanswerable, and angels remain an ineffable foundation upon which our lives and our mission are built.

Writings about angel sightings through history are notoriously unreliable. The general consensus is that angels are shaped like humans, but are much larger, winged, and glowing with heavenly fire—but many authors have suggested that when angels *do* manifest in our world, they take whatever shape witnesses will recognize as angelic. Today the Clave is dubious of claims about angel appearances and mostly declines to investigate them. This attitude has been firmly in place ever since an embarrassing episode in 1832 during which a Prussian farmer and Shadowhunter, Johannes von Mainz, called the entire Clave to his farm to witness the "angel" he had summoned to his cow barn. Awe quickly turned to chagrin when some of the neighbors recognized the "angel" as Johannes's son Hans, covered in gold leaf and bellowing pronouncements in a vulgar mix of Latin, German, and what appears to have been a nonsense language of Hans's own invention. The angel's wings turned out to be a mix of goose, duck, and chicken feathers haphazardly pasted to a wooden frame. Johannes retreated to his farm in humiliation, and Hans was no longer able to so much as go into town without receiving catcalls and being pelted with feathers. Since then most Shadowhunters have been very cautious in either making or checking claims of angel appearances. *Oh, Johannes, what will we do with you?*

Teacher? I did an independent study, does that count?

THE ANGEL RAZIEL

Yes. You may skip this section. Enjoy your newfound sixty seconds.

The Angel Raziel holds, of course, a special role as the patron of the Shadowhunters and the creator of the Nephilim. His role in that creation is discussed thoroughly elsewhere in this volume; here we address what is known about Raziel himself.

Raziel is believed to be of the rank of archangel, within the heavenly chorus. In Jewish mystical traditions he is often called the Keeper of Secrets and the Angel of Mysteries. Interestingly, Jewish mysticism includes what appears to be a distorted version of the Gray Book, known as the Book of Raziel and containing a strange amalgam of kabbalistic teachings, angelology, glosses on the Jewish creation stories, and corrupted forms of demonic incantation. The book also contains a large number of runes, most of them totally invented but some of them corruptions of true Marks (but without any instruction on how they might be used or what their purpose might be). Extant copies of this text exist in both Hebrew and Latin today but only as historical curiosities. The movement during the mundane Renaissance in Europe against magic of all kinds labeled the book a dangerous work of dark magic, and its use was suppressed by mundane religious authorities, to the benefit of the Nephilim.

It is difficult to make any clear statements on Raziel's earthly appearance; we can go only from the earliest art and text describing and depicting the birth of the Nephilim. From that, we can put together, as it were, a composite sketch. We can say that the Angel is consistently depicted as many times the size of a man, as having long hair of silver and gold, as being covered in golden Marks not found in the Gray Book, and as a being whose appearances "fled from the mind and memory as quickly as they were seen." Many depictions show him with large golden wings, each feather of which contains a single golden eye.

Unfortunately, when speaking of the first meeting of the Angel Raziel and Jonathan Shadowhunter, an act of great symbolic as well as actual significance, it is difficult to divide what is intended as factual description from what is meant as allegory. Since history has not preserved a record of this first meeting—as told by Jonathan himself or even by anyone who personally knew Jonathan—all depictions of Raziel must be assumed to have some kernel of truth but also some kernel of interpretive fiction.

What is generally accepted is that Raziel is (a) huge, (b) terrifying, and (c) displeased to be dragged into human affairs, preferring for us to use the tools granted us to solve our own problems. There are many (possibly apocryphal) stories through Nephilim history of unfortunate Shadowhunters attempting to summon Raziel, only to be quickly smote and reduced to ash for wasting the Great Angel's time. The Mortal Instruments are meant to summon Raziel and provide protection so that the summoner will not, in fact, suffer a swift death. Unfortunately, Raziel is unlikely to look kindly upon those who summon him in response to a problem that is not global and truly epic. In addition, the question is merely theoretical, since the Mortal Mirror is lost to the Shadowhunters and has been for hundreds of years.

Seems obvious once you know the secret, huh?

It's a little embarrassing now, I won't lie.

OTHER ANGELS KNOWN TO THE SHADOWHUNTERS

It is a common question among young Nephilim: If angels never appear in our world, and cannot and should not be summoned here, why must we learn and memorize the names of so many of them? Shadowhunters must know the names of the angels, first because we are of their blood and so we learn their names out of respect. Also, of course, we name our seraph blades after them, and it's believed that the seraph blades are infused not just with the generic heavenly fire of *adamas* but with some of the spirit of the named angel. This is why you will rarely find seraph blades named after the most famous and powerful of angels out of worry that such angelic power might overwhelm and destroy the wielder of such a weapon.

Hereafter follows a basic lexicon of angels known to the Shadowhunters, to be used to name seraph blades. More thorough information on each angel can be found in the official angel handbook, *Be Not Afraid*, 1973, Alicante.

A handy tip: When angels say "be not afraid," you should be afraid.

Also, as I said earlier, we have to memorize angel names because Jonathan Shadowhunter wanted us to have to memorize angel names.

120

They sure like to end angel names in "el."

Means "of God" in Hebrew, Clariel.

YOU TWO ARE JUST ADORABLE.

Adriel	Marut
Ambriel	Metatron
Amriel	Michael
Anael	Moroni
Arariel	Munkar
Ariel	Muriel
Asmodei	Nakir
Atheed	Nuriel
Barachiel	Pahaliah
Camael	Penemue
Cassiel	Peniel
Dumah	Puriel
Eremiel	Raguel
Gabriel	Raphael
Gadreel	Raqeeb
Gagiel	Raziel
Hadraniel	Remiel
Haniel	Ridwan
Harahel	Sachiel
Harut	Samandriel
Israfiel	Sandalphon
Ithuriel	Saraqael
Jahoel	Sealtiel
Jegudiel	Shamsiel
Jehuel	Taharial
Jerahmeel	Uriel
Jophiel	Yahoel
Khamael	Zadkiel
Lailah	Zaphkiel
Malik	

Another handy tip: Do not name a seraph blade "Raziel." Legend says he doesn't like it.

What would happen?

121

Just ... don't do it. Nothing good.

DO NOT SUMMON ANGELS

Wait. I'm confused. So I . . . should summon angels? Is that right?

One of the lessons learned most quickly by Shadowhunters is that life is deeply unfair. Most unfair is the truth that while our vocation and mission are given to us by Raziel, we have essentially no direct access to angels or their powers [which we the editors hesitate to refer to as magic; the faculties of angels are rather beyond the ken of even the most powerful warlock, for example]. As a young Shadowhunter you may have considered that the best weapon against the demon threat might be an equal opposing angel threat, and you have thought in your idle moments of summoning an angel yourself. Perhaps you have even sought tales or grimoires on angel summoning in your Institute library.

The Shadowhunter art is an ever evolving one, and yesterday's forbidden methods are tomorrow's accepted norms. However, there is a rule that remains globally true:

You should not attempt to summon an angel to your aid.

There are several major reasons for this. The first, and least interesting, is that it is most likely a waste of your time. Angels do not respond to summonings in the same way that demons do. For one thing, they cannot maintain a corporeal form in our dimension for long, any more than other non-demon creatures can in a dimension not their own. And the summoning rituals that claim to bring angels to us are obscure, difficult, and unreliable; they have been accomplished so rarely that we don't have much evidence for what does and does not work. The risk of disaster, injury, or death from a misunderstood or misapplied summoning ritual is very high.

The second reason not to attempt an angel summoning is that there is no way to oblige an angel to cooperate with your needs. An angel cannot be *bound* in the way that a demon is bound, except by the application of forbidden and blasphemous rituals; the

122

performance of which are among the worst violations of Law that a Shadowhunter could commit.

Finally, even if a summoning is successful, you and any companions you persuade to assist you will die, and die quickly. Unlike demons, angels do not *want* to be on our plane of reality. They do not like manifesting here, they do not like helping humans, and they are not known for their mercy. They are on the whole deeply indifferent to the travails of the mortal realm. They are not merely messengers but soldiers: Michael is said to have routed armies. They are not patient or tolerant of human vicissitudes. You must put out of your head images of naked winged babies draping someone in robes. Angels are great and terrible. They are our allies, yes, but make no mistake: They are utterly alien and inhuman. They are, in fact, far more inhuman than the most monstrous demon you will encounter. Angel blood we may carry in our veins, yes, but pure heavenly fire will burn and consume us, as surely as demonic poison will.

Angels are our mystical source of power, and the origin of whatever righteousness we possess. They are not, however, our friends. *Yes, yes, ha ha, it's all very funny, this is actually important advice here.*

ON ANGEL BLOOD *What are the odds this is going to come up again?!*

Nephilim are raised knowing that in their veins flows some of the blood of angels, and thus angel blood is a substance about which many stories and tall tales have been told— that it grants superior strength, that it cures any disease, that it lengthens the human life. All of these claims must be considered less than credible, if only because stories claiming the appearance of angels in our world are, to our knowledge, universally false. A Downworlder who claims to be selling angel blood, or anything derived from angel blood, is lying to you. Shadowhunters should be too smart to be taken in by such claims, but sadly over the years a number of young Nephilim have shaken in Institute infirmaries, recovering from the ingestion of whatever substances have been mixed together to give the semblance of angel blood. There are no vials of angel blood floating around that grant superpowers. None. Do not fall for this ruse. *Ahem.*

I guess this is another one where I get credit for real-life experience.

I believe so, yes.

— MUNDANES —

Oh, I can't wait.

The mundane world is the world you know. It is the world from which, new Nephilim, you have come, and its people, the mundanes, are the people you knew and the people you yourself were, until recently when you were changed. We often speak of the mundane world as though it is a minor aspect of our lives and our world, but in truth we exist by necessity *because* of mundanes. When Nephilim say we are protectors of the world, what we mean is protectors of the mundanes. They are our charges and our responsibility. *Chumps!*

Mundanes live their lives in ignorance of the shadows surrounding them, and it is our job to protect that ignorance and, as much as possible, maintain it. As you walk the streets of your cities and towns, as you patrol, you will be surrounded by mundanes living their lives, celebrating and mourning, knocked about by happiness and sadness and anger and sorrow and joy. These emotions you see may be at odds with what you, with the true Sight, know to be the truth. Sometimes drastically at odds. Many are the Nephilim who have been shaken by their need to run down and fight to exhaustion a demon who threatens to destroy an entire town of smiling, oblivious mundanes. This is one of the burdens we bear. It is our job to bear it appropriately.

Mundanes are, of course, not allowed into Idris, or into any Institute, under normal circumstances. The Law allows for Shadowhunters to offer mundanes sanctuary if they are in imminent danger from a demon or Downworlder attack, or danger from the results of a demon or Downworlder attack. Note that the Law does not *obligate* Shadowhunters to do this. The Nephilim's holy mission is to protect mundanes, but not at the expense of our own safety. Shadowhunters must judge whether a mundane can be given sanctuary without compromising the larger secrecy, and therefore safety, of the Shadow World.

It is easy to feel contempt, and even envy, for mundanes. They are, after all, in danger from a demonic threat of which they know nothing. They go about their lives complacently; they have the luxury of not knowing the truth of the great battle of good and evil that looms over their world constantly. They have the luxury of not being in a state of constant war, of knowing that each of your friends, of your family members, is in battle every day from which, every day, there is a chance they might not return.

125

We urge you: Have compassion for the mundane world. It is our lot to fight for them and for them not to know of our sacrifices. This is not their fault. *Oh, come on, it's not that bad.*

THOSE POOR BASTARDS. I PITY THEM. JUST . . . PITY THEM. *They want us to be kind to mundanes!*

MUNDANES WHO ARE NOT ENTIRELY MUNDANE

THEY ARE SOMEWHAT COOL. BUT NOT AS COOL AS SHADOWHUNTERS.

Lays it on a little thick though. SHADOWHUNTER DOTH PROTEST TOO MUCH, METHINKS.

There are, of course, mundanes who are not entirely mundane— *Methinks too.* whose families have, somewhere in their history, faerie blood, or werewolf blood, or even, rarely, Nephilim blood. This blood persists through generations, and these mundanes may be identified by having the Sight and by being able to see through some glamours. (Most, however, still never notice any supernatural activity, because they are not prepared to see it. An important rule of glamours: For the most part people see what they wish to see. (See "Glamours and the Sight," page 140.) Even Sighted mundanes will often look past strange appearances and explain them as illusions or misunderstandings.)

Many of these mundane-yet-Sighted families used to act as the servants and caretakers of various Institutes and wealthy Shadowhunter families; however, in most parts of the world, the practice of keeping servants has long gone out of fashion, and these families have ceased their relationships with the Nephilim. Several generations have passed since this happened in North America and Europe, and most living members of these families no longer even know that their ancestors once served the Nephilim.

Even those mundanes who do not possess the Sight may often find themselves drawn to places of magic and power, though they will not understand why. Sometimes they will find themselves compelled to make some physical mark on such a place—to build barriers separating it from the places around it, to decorate it, even to deface or vandalize it. This can be annoying to Nephilim and

Downworlders who need to make use of these sites of power, but again we urge you to have patience and pity for these mundanes. There must be some magic deep within the collective memory of all humans, for otherwise how could we (and Downworlders) make use of any magic, even with the addition of angel or demon blood? We must, all of us, have at least the *potential* to be of the Nephilim. That magic spills out into all the world, and it is part of our responsibility as Shadowhunters to maintain it.

(See also: "Mundane Demonic Cults," page 75.) JUST YOUR EVERYDAY RUN-OF-THE-mill DEMONIC CULT.

A NOTE ON MUNDANE RELIGION

Many new Shadowhunters come to us from their own religious history and want to know which religion is "right." This knowledge is not something that Shadowhunters possess any more than mundanes do. Shadowhunters proudly originate from all points of the globe, and we naturally see and think about the Shadow World within the context of our personal beliefs.

This diversity may seem like a weakness, keeping Shadowhunters separated from one another, just as mundanes are by their beliefs. But these mundane religions have much to teach us. Encased in their mythologies and legends are practical truths about angels, demons, perhaps even Downworlders. We include all of them in our researches.

Also, mundane religion represents the moral and ethical beliefs, and spiritual insights, of our species, and we have much to learn from these as well. We ignore the teachings of the wisest of mundanes at our peril. If *all the stories are true*, we must remember that those stories have mostly been written down by mundanes.

The world's religions always have assisted, and will continue to assist, the Nephilim in our mission. Religious communities and holy buildings are universally available as havens for Shadow-hunters, and often contain secret caches of weapons and tools for Shadowhunter use. The agreements concerning these caches often go back five hundred or more years. In fact, the oldest continually operating Nephilim weapons cache in the world can be found in Milan—one of the largest mundane trade cities closest to Idris—in the Basilica di Sant'Ambrogio. The Milanese Nephilim claim that this cache was established by Jonathan Shadowhunter himself, late in his life, in what was then the new bell tower of the church.

Traditionally, entrance to caches was effected by the recitation of the so-called Martyr's Creed:

In the name of the Clave, I ask entry to this holy place.
In the name of the Battle That Never Ends, I ask the use of your weapons. And in the name of the Angel Raziel, I ask your blessings on my mission against the darkness.

Today most caches follow the more expedient method of open-ing to the presence of a Voyance rune, but the traditional method still works in most places, for those Shadowhunters who prefer a little more drama.

I actually have to memorize that, don't I. I've heard Jace say it. Yep. You have to memorize a million Marks, too, you know.

But that is eeeeasy
This is haaaard.

—— THE FORSAKEN ——

THERE'S NO WHINING IN SHADOWHUNTERING
Oh, you know that's not tr—

It was only shortly after the creation of the first Nephilim that humanity came to know, to its detriment, what happens if you Mark a person who does not have Shadowhunter blood, or who has not been made a Shadowhunter by drinking from the Mortal Cup. A single Mark is likely only to cause a burning pain where

Okay. Here's my question, Codex. Why did Valentine stop using Forsaken? Why doesn't every bad guy create a giant Forsaken army?

it has been inscribed on the skin, but a number of Marks—and it does not take many—will drive a mundane to agonizing pain and mindless, insane rage. The Mortal Cup, or inherited Shadowhunter blood, steels the body against the overwhelming strength of angelic power that flows through the Marks, but an unprepared mortal will die.

They do not eat or sleep, and they ignore their injuries and wounds. As a result they are short-lived creatures, and it is only a matter of chance whether they are killed off first by starvation, exhaustion, or infection.

IF YOU MEET A FORSAKEN

Killing Forsaken is, in short, a mercy. Do not, however, take on a Forsaken one-on-one. It is easy to underestimate their strength and cunning. If necessary, flee and return with backup.

The only known method of ending the agony of a Forsaken,

129

other than killing him, is to make him drink from the Mortal Cup, whose power will eliminate the unfathomable pain of the Marks. Technically this will turn the Forsaken into a full Shadowhunter. There are, however, zero recorded cases in which the sufferer survived the dual shock of becoming Forsaken and then becoming Nephilim, so it is best to consider them beyond help.

WHERE DID FORSAKEN COME FROM?

We cannot know the horror of the first Forsaken, whose story is lost to history, but it must have been early in the spread of Nephilim through the world. As early as the mid-1200s, not long after the believed death of Jonathan Shadowhunter, we have notes from the Silent City suggesting that the Brothers were seeking a cure for the Forsaken. Forsaken are mentioned by that name in the first written version of Covenant Law, by the first Consul, Edward the Good and Ready, and are condemned as illegal and in fact blasphemous.

The real problem with Forsaken is that in their madness they are dangerously suggestible, and they have some affinity for the one who has Marked them. This enables the wielder of the Mark to command them. They can be made to survive for longer than normal by being ordered by their master to eat, drink, and sleep, and they can understand other simple commands. They are thus occasionally used as slave labor, but their unending rage and pain make them mostly useful only for committing violence. Forsaken are unable to build or construct anything, and they are unable to speak.

There have been surprisingly few attacks by Forsaken recorded in our history. They are certainly a threat to mundanes, but they are not actually very strong. Despots do not raise Forsaken armies, because Forsaken make terrible soldiers: They can't wield weapons, and they can't implement tactics or defend themselves. They are much less intelligent than human soldiers, and they require the same resources to maintain. They are easily neutralized as a threat by prepared Nephilim, or indeed by a powerful warlock or a significant force of werewolves or vampires. Because of all of these aspects, most Forsaken we know of were the result of errors, such as a mundane foolishly trying to turn himself into a Shadowhunter. There have also been isolated occasions in which being made Forsaken was used as a punishment, but it has always been against Nephilim Law to do so, and those Shadowhunters who were caught doing this would have been arrested and imprisoned in the Silent City for their crime.

Note that we do not see parallel "demonic Forsaken." Demonic magic, of course, has its own runes that could be theoretically inscribed on a person's flesh. In practice, though, these runes tend to produce an effect not unlike a strong demon poison. Thus we do not find, say, warlocks using them to enhance themselves; these runes cause not the mindless rage and pain of the Forsaken but the wasting collapse of the poisoned and are of no real use in practice.

Well, ten points to you, Codex. You answered my question: no Forsaken army because they fall apart and they are really stupid. Fair enough.

—— GHOSTS AND THE DEAD ——

Ghosts and spirits rarely appear in usual Shadowhunter business, but nevertheless for many Nephilim the Sight includes the ability to see, hear, and speak with the spirits of the dead. You may have it yourself! This aspect of the Sight is entirely hereditary and cannot be enhanced with Marks.

Even those Shadowhunters who cannot actually speak to or see the forms of ghosts can nevertheless usually sense their presence nearby, by noting the existence of an unnatural cold feeling. When

131

ghosts manifest themselves in our world, they must draw energy from around them in order to maintain their ectoplasmic form, and thus suck the heat from their surroundings.

The strongest ghosts may in fact be able to manifest themselves into a close semblance of life. We can, however, always tell a ghost by its eyes: They will be hollow and empty.

Sometimes, in the case of the strongest spirits, the eyes will have flames flickering in their depths, but this is fairly rare.

The prevailing theory of ghosts is that they are trapped in our world by some wrong or crime they are seeking to resolve; they are literally "restless" and seek the talisman that will allow them to pass out of our world and into theirs fully. It takes a certain amount of strength for a ghost to be aware enough of itself and its former life to identify its talisman, and ghosts have no magical knowledge of what that talisman might be or what act might put them to rest; they are, in most cases, just guessing, and may be wrong, or too demented to accurately comprehend their situation.

WAIT WAIT WAIT, WE COULD HAVE BEEN DEALING WITH GHOSTS ALL THIS TIME TOO?
WHERE ARE THE GHOSTS? BRING ON THE GHOSTS! You don't actually want that. New York has some bad ghosts. Trust me.

Things to ask Jace about the existence of

You left this blank. What do you want to know about?

The book leaves a bunch of things out! Like mummies. Tell me about mummi

Mummies exist. The Egyptians mummified people.
Mummies that get up out of their cursed tombs and walk around do not exist.

Do cursed tombs exist?

No. Sometimes you get a tomb guarded by a demon.

Zombies?

The voudun kind, yes—the braaaaaaiiiiiinnnnsss kind, no

OH, OH, I'VE GOT ONE. WHAT ABOUT A HAUNTED CAR?
CAN YOU HAVE A HAUNTED CAR?

Do you count a demon-powered motorcycle?

No, LIKE, THE CAR TALKS TO YOU AND TELLS YOU TO KILL PEOPLE.

Then no.

BESTIAIRE PART III: ANGELS AND MEN

DISCUSSION QUESTIONS AND THINGS TO TRY

Why am I even answering you? You are not a Shadowhunter. No, no leprechauns.

Elder gods?

Jace is ignoring Simon. Elder gods. Jace—same question.

1. Do you come to the Shadowhunters with existing religious beliefs? Try reading some of the Shadowhunter scholars of your religion from the past, who will help you learn how to fit your new knowledge of the Shadow World into your worldview.

We'd just consider them Greater Demons, I think.

TRANSFORMERS!

I will get right on that. _____

I don't know what those are.

ALIEN ROBOTS THAT TURN INTO OTHER THINGS THAT DON'T LOOK LIKE ROBOTS!

2. Can you see ghosts? If so, try to find a haunting near you. Someone in your Institute will know of one. Describe your spectral experience here.

I cannot see ghosts. I am actually pretty happy about that.

3. SERIOUSLY, HOW MUCH DO MUNDANES SUCK? So much.

Mundane rights!

Also, what about Smurfs? Also, and I am totally serious here, Santa Claus?

I can't believe I am defending the Clave, but really, guys, this section is pretty good by their standards.

CHAPTER SIX

GRIMOIRE

— AN INTRODUCTORY NOTE — ON MAGIC

Nephilim do not perform magic.

This is—far and away—the thing that most separates us from both demons and Downworlders. Demons perform magic—indeed, the vast majority of magic that you will see in the world is demonic in origin. The powers given to werewolves and vampires, too, are demonic magic. Faerie magic is the great unknown—it is very different from the magic of demons, but some believe that the two have the same origin.

Whatever the case, the Nephilim do not have any magic of their own. We use, rather, magical tools that have been gifted to us by higher powers. We cannot make new Marks. We have access only to the ones that were handed to us in the Gray Book. We can experiment with their use, but they are all the power we have been granted. Everything else that Nephilim are we have made on our own. *Most of us cannot make new Marks, that is.*

Through history many Nephilim, especially Silent Brothers, have spent countless thousands of hours trying to discover the underlying "language" and "grammar" of angelic Marks. If their constituent parts could be understood, it was believed, then perhaps new Marks could be created. These projects have inevitably led to failure. If there is an elemental grammar of Marks, then it seems that we humans are not permitted to know it, or are not capable of discovering it.

By comparison, demon magic is a much broader and more

According to Jace: weird Nephilim Pride stuff here. Most Shadowhunters don't care that much.

137

powerful magic in all its forms—whether wielded directly by demons or warlocks, or whether installed in the souls of vampires or lycanthropes. Faerie magic is more powerful still.

This is a lesson never to be forgotten by any Shadowhunter: We are outmatched. We are outgunned. What keeps us is our determination, our oath, our adherence to Law, our discipline, and our training.

—— WHY? ——

The great question of the Nephilim, the great mystery left unanswered by Raziel and unasked by Jonathan Shadowhunter, is this: Why have we been left with such limited powers? Why have the Downworlders been given such a range of superhuman abilities—immortality, strength, and speed beyond their physical bodies, the ability to invent and create new magic—when we have been given such limited and unchangeable weapons for our fight?

This is a question without an answer, and in fact to suggest a definitive answer is to presume to know the minds of angels. Let us, however, suggest that the Shadowhunter hold within her mind two qualities of great warriors—that of dignity and that of humility.

Dignity: Our power is that we are *chosen*. Unlike demons, born of the Void and without the free will to choose aught but evil; or Downworlders, whose powers are so often the result of accidents of birth, unpredictable events, terrible crimes; we have been selected to bear the blood of angels and lead the fight against Hell.

And humility: We are dust and ashes. We are mortal. We are vulnerable. We bleed and we die.

And in these two extremes is our great strength and our great frailty. *This: Cheesy but true! This kind of describes all people. We count as people!*

BASIC INTERDIMENSIONAL SPACE-TIME THEORY *Do I even have to say you can skip this sidebar?*

So far you know of two worlds: the mundane world and the Shadow World. But there are worlds other than these. Our world overlaps with others, infinitely many others, that are separate from our world yet occupy the same space, in an alternate reality. These alternate realities have no obligation to hew to the same rules that our own universe follows, and so it's generally assumed that we could not survive in most of them. Not only need they not have things such as water and air and a temperature that we can stand, but they need not have the same physical laws or forms of life, and in these worlds we might disintegrate, unable to sustain our existence in a universe totally hostile to it.

What, I didn't hear you. I was busy skipping this sidebar.

Some believe Faerie to be a dimension different from our world (see discussion of the fey, Bestiaire Part II, Chapter 4), but we know for sure that the Void, home of the demons, is a different dimension. Attempts to follow demons home through their Portals back to the Void have proved to be instantly fatal to humans. It's suspected that angels come from yet another dimension, but this is mere speculation.

In truth we don't know whether the Void is a single alternate dimension—or many dimensions, or even an infinitude of dimensions whose nexus lies at

Pandemonium. In practice it does not much matter. Our vocation as Nephilim is to protect our own dimension; we will allow other universes to take care of themselves.

You shouldn't have skipped it. This is cool stuff. Space-time! Dimensions! More of this kind of thing please, thanks, love Simon.

—— GLAMOURS AND THE SIGHT ——

A glamour is the simplest magic in existence. It makes things look different from how they are. Performed correctly, it creates a perfect semblance in the mind of the observer and perfectly obscures the true shape of the thing glamoured. It is one of the few kinds of magic available to all known magic users—it is found in the Gray Book, in demonic spell books, in the researches of warlocks, and among the fey. And a glamour is the most widely and extensively used magic because of its necessity: It hides the Shadow World from mundanes, a goal that all of that world agrees upon.

Most glamours are easy to see through for any magical being, and they usually hide things only from mundanes. Vampires, faeries, and warlocks all may use more powerful glamours to hide their activities not just from mundanes but also from Shadowhunters and from one another. Faeries especially are considered the masters of glamour magic; some Nephilim theorize that everything we see of Faerie in this world is modified by a glamour in some way.

Glamours are most commonly used to put a false skin over something, as with the glamours we place on our Institutes. Nephilim also often glamour ourselves into invisibility, to move undetected through the mundane world. This is significantly easier than glamouring gear into the semblance of street clothes, weapons into the semblance of harmless tools, and so on. Similarly,

demons may glamour themselves into nonspecific forms, so that a mundane attacked by a demon will perceive it as something generic, like a dog or another random mundane.

The ability to see past glamours to a thing's true nature is often called the Sight, a term from mundane folklore. Most Shadowhunters are born with the Sight, inherited from their Shadowhunter parents. All Shadowhunters typically enhance their Sight with the permanent application of a Voyance rune, because Sight is the *only* means of seeing through glamours. Just knowing that something has been glamoured, or even knowing its true shape, does not remove the glamour effect.

This is notable because there are many folk beliefs among mundane cultures about rituals and tools that can be used to see through glamours. Some of these may successfully work to help us see through faerie glamours, by means we do not understand. These tools—clary sage, Seeing Stones, wearing clothing inside out, washing your face in a particular spring at sunrise, and so on—cannot, however, be used to see through the more common glamours used by warlocks, demons, and Shadowhunters.

Some mundanes do naturally possess true Sight, usually credited to fey blood in their ancestry, though no direct connection has ever been proved.

WHAT IS A GLAMOUR?

The origin of glamour magic is a subject that has puzzled generations of magical researchers—how is it that all of the Shadow World has access to it, and are the different versions related? There have been various theories, the most common of which historically has been that glamour magic originally belonged to the fey and was "stolen" from them by other creatures somehow. It's not clear how this could have happened, though, and so the prevailing theory today is that there are at root two types of glamours—the angelic glamours that we Nephilim use, produced by the inscription of Marks, and demonic glamours, used by everyone else. It's assumed that Raziel granted us the power of glamours, just as he granted us the power of Sight, to put us on an even footing with our foes, and to allow us to protect ourselves from mundane discovery.

I did not know this, but it turned out to be because I did not care.

——— ANGELIC MAGIC ———

THE MORTAL INSTRUMENTS

The Mortal Instruments are the greatest gifts entrusted to the Nephilim. Without them there are no Shadowhunters, no Marks used by humans, and no recourse against the demonic threat. The Instruments are venerated by Shadowhunters as our most sacred relics and are given to the Silent Brothers to keep and protect.

It is believed that the Mortal Instruments have functions beyond those that we know; old writings, especially among the Silent Brothers, speak obscurely of angelic powers essential to the Instruments that could be wielded if only we knew what they

were. These powers remain ineffable to us. Sadly, no use has ever been found for the Cup or the Sword beyond those enumerated below, and, of course, we do not know what power, if any, the Mirror might possess.

The power of dunking you in a lake and then driving you mad.

THE CUP *Well done there. So glad we know about that now.*

The Mortal Cup is the means by which Nephilim are created. It is often called Raziel's Cup, or the Cup of the Angel. As our legends tell us, the Angel Raziel presented himself to Jonathan Shadowhunter and filled the cup with a mixture of his own angelic ichor and Jonathan's mundane blood. Jonathan drank from the cup and became the first Nephilim. Thereafter the Cup was imbued with angelic power, and drinking holy liquid from it would transform a mundane into a Nephilim.

The Cup is not as ornate and decorative as most new Shadowhunters assume. No jewel-encrusted chalice, it is the size of only an ordinary wineglass, and it is dipped in unadorned gold. It is carved from *adamas*, which is much heavier than glass. It is unusual that the Cup was gilded, considering the essential holiness of *adamas*—which to Shadowhunters is holier than gold.

Its *adamas* construction, however, is not the source of its power, any more than its gilding. It is assumed that the Cup is made of *adamas* because that is the angels' metal, unbreakable by any substance on earth (except the sacred fires of the Adamant Citadel). It is generally believed that Raziel could have made any cup into the Mortal Cup. It became sacred when the Angel used it as the vessel for his blood.

There have been periods of history in which the Cup was in frequent use by the Clave, but in the past fifty years this practice has mostly died out. The 1950s saw a large expansion of Shadowhunter families across the world, mostly to replenish the ranks of Nephilim lost in major world conflicts, but the Clave then saw a period of relative stability, and the current Shadowhunter families were considered sufficient to fill our ranks.

The worst use of the Mortal Cup, historically, was during the Hunts, when it was used for a form of inquisitional torture and murder. Downworlders, of course, cannot drink from the Cup and cannot bear Marks. They will typically, if given to drink from the Cup, vomit up its contents, but if they are forced to continue to drink from the vessel, it will soon burn the life out of them entirely, and they will die in paroxysms of suffering as the demonic and angelic war fruitlessly within them. (This fate is similar to that of the offspring of a demon and Shadowhunter, who cannot survive to birth.) This method of capital punishment was considered by some Shadowhunters—and, shamefully, the Clave as a whole for a time—to be not only just but merciful, since it infused the Downworlder with angelic power before death. Now viewed as barbaric and torturous, the practice fell off in most parts of the world in the early eighteenth century. It was eliminated as an official form of punishment by Consul Suleiman Kanuni in 1762 but was only made fully illegal in the Second Accords of 1887. *This is terrible! Why must you tell me these terrible things, Codex? I just wanted to learn about the Cup. At least they admit*

THE SWORD *to doing it and agree it was bad. That's a big step for the Clave.*

The Mortal Sword, often called the Soul-Sword, is the second of the Mortal Instruments. It resides in the Silent City and normally is hung above the Speaking Stars in the Silent Brothers' council chamber. When it is needed, it is typically wielded by Silent Brothers. Its primary use is to compel Nephilim to tell only truth. As Raziel said, the Sword cuts the knot of lies and deceptions to reveal the golden truth beneath. It is used in modern times mostly during trials, to compel honest testimony from witnesses, those who would have a vested interest in lying. Shadowhunters who wish to have their claims tested and proved may submit themselves to "trial by the Sword." In this process a suitable judge—usually a Silent Brother—"wields" the sword by placing it in the hands of the deponent, where it adheres and from whence it cannot be removed until the judge wills it.

Neither Downworlders nor mundanes can be compelled by the Soul-Sword. This limit is believed to have been placed purposefully, to prevent the Shadowhunters from using the Sword as a general tool of interrogation. It is intended to maintain the integrity and honor of the Nephilim ourselves, and not to be a weapon wielded against others.

It is assumed that the Sword will not work on demons or angels, but this has never been tested. Since the fey are unable to speak untruths in the first place, its use on them would be redundant.

The Sword's shape is more or less typical of an arming sword or a knightly sword of Jonathan Shadowhunter's period. (It is believed that Raziel would have produced, in the Mortal Instruments, weapons and items that would have been somewhat familiar to Jonathan, so that their intention for use by humans would be clear.) It has a one-handed hilt and a straight double-edged blade. Unlike most Western swords of the period, it does not have a cruciform hilt but rather an elaborate design of outspread wings, emerging from the point where blade meets handle. Here the sword's heavenly origin is clear; the details of the sword are significantly more intricate and flawless than any human artisan could produce. *See, that was better. No one was unexpectedly tortured and murdered.*

THE MIRROR *Except in real life, by Valentine, using that sword. Remember?*
The Mirror, also sometimes called the Mortal Glass, is the great mystery of the legend of Jonathan Shadowhunter. It is clearly the third of the Mortal Instruments given by Raziel, and it is mentioned in all Shadowhunter histories, so we do not believe that it is a later addition. No specifics, however, are given about

more of that, is what I am saying.

146

the Mirror—where it resides, what it looks like, or even its intended function. There have been many searches for the Mirror in our history, in excavations and old libraries, through crypts and ancient Shadowhunter ruins—none of them successful. There have also, of course, been many false Mirrors that have been claimed as real, either by charlatans seeking power among the Nephilim or by naive and hopeful Shadowhunters desperate for an answer to the riddle.

Legend tells us that Raziel can be summoned by the use of the Mortal Instruments: One must hold the Cup and the Sword and stand before the Mirror. This claim must, however, remain but a story, since the Mortal Glass is lost to our knowledge, perhaps lost entirely to time. *You know what is weird? When this came out, the Cup was lost. No one knew where it was. People thought it was gone for good. No mention here at all!*

THE MARKS OF RAZIEL

Official position was "temporarily misplaced." The Codex is about as official as it gets. That is ridiculous.

The most common tools of the Shadowhunter, the source of our ability to fight the demonic Incursion at all, are of course the Marks of Raziel, the complex runic language given to us by the Angel to grant us powers beyond mundanes. You will learn these Marks for yourself—it is one of the most important tasks of your training. No one person knows *every* Mark, of course, but you will begin with the most common and useful, and will gradually learn more as they become useful or necessary to you.

Hey, we got the Cup back, didn't we? So they were right!

Learning Marks can be difficult, especially for Shadowhunters from Western countries. Many beginning students, and especially Westerners, will tend to think of Marks as a discrete set of "powers"—spells from a spell book that you have to memorize how to draw. Those Shadowhunters who are from cultures that use logographic written language, such as China, Vietnam, or the

Yes yes, you're some kind of Marks savant, you don't really need to worry about these. Check to make sure you know all of them, I guess.

All of them?

All of them.

147

Mayan Empire, may have an easier time absorbing the truth—that the angelic Marks are a language that we as humans cannot know in the particulars of its grammar. But we can acquire an intuitive sense of the relationships among the Marks that can make the learning experience more like becoming fluent in a language and less like memorizing a list of symbols. As with all other human talents, some Nephilim are naturally skilled at this, and some must work harder to gain competence.

We are restricted in our power in that we are permitted to use only the runes found in the Gray Book. There are demonic runes—possibly multiple different demonic runic languages—that are forbidden to us, by Law and also because they cannot work alongside the seraphic blood of the Nephilim. We cannot understand the underlying language of the Marks we have, and thus we cannot create new angelic Marks. But there are also other angelic runes, we know not how many, that have existed since time immemorial and that are, for whatever reasons, not given to us for our use. The most well-known of these is the so-called first Mark, the Mark of Cain, the first time that Heaven chose to Mark a human and provide protection. It is easy to see the origin of our magic in the first of all murderers as a dire omen, to see the affiliation as one we would prefer not to have. Yet we would argue the opposite: The Mark of Cain is a Mark of protection. It tells us that the justice of Heaven is not absolute and that this justice still contains the possibility of compassion and mercy.

Represent! Compassion and mercy! Booyah!

THE GRAY BOOK

Please never say "booyah" again.

The *Book of Gramarye* is the official name for the book of Marks that all Shadowhunters learn from. Each copy exactly replicates the contents of the original book of the Covenant in which the Angel Raziel inscribed the Marks given to Jonathan Shadowhunter. Unlike many other such holy books that claim exact replication

148

through history, the Gray Book's quality is maintained by a built-in check: in any given copy, all the Marks must work as drawn! This, and the continuity of Shadowhunter authority across the years, has allowed us to speak with confidence in saying that the Gray Book represents, indeed, the language of Raziel.

Preparing pages to hold the runes involves some complex magical legerdemain, which makes the process of creating a Gray Book an arduous one, always performed by Silent Brothers. Because of this complexity, the binding is often decorative and highly ornamented, to celebrate the effort involved in creating the interior. Institutes and a few old Shadowhunter families guard their Gray Books carefully and pass them down through the generations, often with much ceremony.

RUNIC MANUSCRIPTION

Learning Marks can be an intimidating process for young Nephilim; invoking the power of Heaven and likely failing the first few times is an understandably unnerving experience. The risks are, however, relatively low. In most cases poorly drawn Marks will have no effect at all and can be removed with no consequences. Most new Shadowhunters at some point perform the experiment of drawing randomly on themselves or on objects with their steles. This will cause the same "icy hot" feeling on the skin that actual Marks bring about, but no other consequences. Similarly, a mundane must be inscribed with actual Marks, and not just random stele sketching, in order to be turned into a Forsaken. One of the first tricks most young Nephilim learn, in fact, is to take advantage of the neutral character of non-Marks and inscribe an incomplete Mark on themselves, which can then be quickly completed and activated at the moment it is needed.

Only Shadowhunters can create Marks. A mundane or Downworlder can hold a stele, and it will not hurt them, but they cannot use it to create Marks; no lines will appear from the end of the stele, no matter what surface it is drawn against. Among Shadowhunters the strength of a given Mark is based on the inscribing Shadowhunter's talent for runic magic. That is, a rune to hold against pursuit will do so in relation to the strength and accuracy of its Mark.

Some Marks are applied to the bodies of Shadowhunters, and some are applied to physical objects. It is usually not dangerous to draw a body Mark on an inanimate object—a rock that has been given the Voyance rune will remain the same inanimate rock it was before. Applying object Marks to a Shadowhunter is somewhat more dangerous, as they will apply to the person's body as a physical object. This is occasionally useful. Note that Marks intended for inanimate objects, like all Marks, cannot be placed on mundanes or Downworlders, as the usual risks of madness, death, or becoming Forsaken still apply.

A Mark's power can be minimized or broken by the Mark's being disfigured. Shadowhunters should pay special attention to this potential target on their bodies; some more intelligent and well-informed foes may attempt to burn or cut Marked skin in order to deprive a Shadowhunter of the benefits of those Marks.

WHAT HAPPENS IF YOU MARK A DEAD BODY?

Nothing.

REALLY? NOTHING UNDEAD OR CREEPY?

Nope.

WELL. I AM DISAPPOINTED.

SPECIFIC MARKS

It is a common misconception that the only Marks used by Shadowhunters are those of battle. While we are warriors—and as such, conflict is part of our lives—we also make use of many Marks that speak in gentler tones. There are Marks for funerals, that tell of healing, grief, and comfort, and there are Marks for celebration, that tell of joy and gratitude. And, of course, there are the Marks that most Nephilim will never encounter, those arcane runes accessible only to Silent Brothers and other runes accessible only to Iron Sisters.

All Marks have names in the Gray Book; only the most common are typically referred to by their true names—*iratze*, for instance—rather than by informal descriptive names (e.g., "strength rune"). But the names of Marks are meaningful: They are in the language of Heaven and are, in fact, the only words of the language of Heaven we have ever been permitted to know. They are our most direct communication with the angels who gave us our lives and our mission.

There are literally thousands of Marks. We offer here a sampling of their designs and basic functions, but the Codex should not be used as a definitive source from which to learn runic manuscription. Please consult the Gray Book and your tutors for help.

Some of the Marks you will likely want to learn early in your education include:

- *The Voyance Mark*—This is the most basic and permanent Shadowhunter Mark, found on essentially all Nephilim, typically on the back of the right hand. It serves to focus the Sight and enable Shadowhunters to see through glamours and, with training and practice, to identify Downworlders on sight.
- *Opening Marks*—There are several variations on these, and it would be wise to learn a few of them before you begin

your active duty. These Marks ensure that no mundane lock, in theory, is closed to the Nephilim. Unfortunately, this also means that many demons and Downworlders will shut things away behind more magical locks.

- *The Tracking Marks*—Another set of indispensable runes for the pursuit of demons, these Marks are easy to learn to draw but difficult to use correctly. They are used as follows: An object possessed by the subject to be tracked is held in a fist in the non-stele hand. Then the tracking rune is drawn on the back of the hand. If the rune is used successfully, the Shadowhunter should see visions of the subject's location. Usually these visions will be accompanied by a knowing sense of orientation: Even if the place seen is unfamiliar, the tracker will have the knowledge of where it is, and in what direction it lies. (A common question about this process: What defines "possession" of an object? "Possession" is here defined literally. Someone is understood to possess something if they can be said to own it or if it is within the place where they live. Thus someone who has sold their house and its furnishings to a new occupant cannot be tracked using those furnishings, which are now in the possession of the new occupant.)
- *Healing Marks*—There are also several of these to be learned. The first is the *iratze*, the basic healing rune, which closes cuts and wounds in Shadowhunters. Note that this means that an *iratze* is not always the best treatment for an injury—for instance, if the Mark would cause the skin to heal over an embedded claw or thorn that needed to be removed. The *iratze* also raises the body temperature temporarily, helping to burn out infection in much the same way a fever does. This rune

TABLE OF SELECTED MARKS

ABUNDANCE	ACCELERATION	ACCURACY
ACTION	AGILITY	AGONY
ANGELIC POWER	AWARENESS	BIND TO

TABLE OF SELECTED MARKS

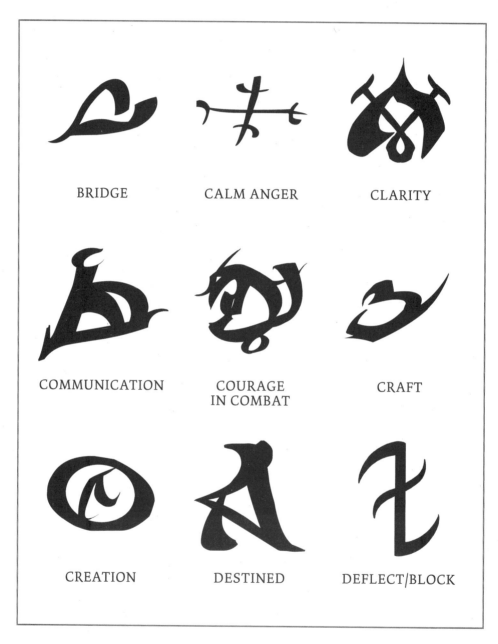

BRIDGE

CALM ANGER

CLARITY

COMMUNICATION

COURAGE
IN COMBAT

CRAFT

CREATION

DESTINED

DEFLECT/BLOCK

TABLE OF SELECTED MARKS

ENDURANCE

ENLIGHTEN

EQUILIBRIUM

EXPECTATION

FIREPROOF

FLEXIBILITY

FORTITUDE

FORTUNE

FRIENDSHIP

TABLE OF SELECTED MARKS

GIFT   GOOD LUCK   GUIDANCE

HEAT   HEIGHTENED SPEED   INSIGHT/
                                       FORESIGHT

IRATZE-HEAL   KNOWLEDGE   LOYAL TO

TABLE OF SELECTED MARKS

MANIFEST

MENTAL EXCELLENCE

MNEMOSYNE

NOURISHMENT

OPPORTUNITY

PERSEVERE

PERSUADE

POWER

PRECISION

TABLE OF SELECTED MARKS

PROMISE

PROSPERITY

PROTECTED

QUIETUDE

RECALL

REMEMBRANCE/
MOURNING

SHARING

SOUNDLESS

SPEAK IN TONGUES

TABLE OF SELECTED MARKS

STAMINA

STEALTH

STRENGTH

SUCCESS

SURE STRIKING

SUREFOOTED

SWIFT

TALENT

TECHNIQUE

TABLE OF SELECTED MARKS

TRANSMISSION

TRUE NORTH

TRUST

UNDERSTANDING

UNSEEN

TABLE OF SELECTED MARKS

VISIBLE

VISION

VOYANCE

WATERPROOF

WEDDED UNION

WINGED

is mostly ineffective against demon poisons and injuries caused by demonic runes. In these cases the injured should be quickly brought to a Silent Brother, but in the meantime it can be useful to apply a *mendelin* rune, which strengthens the victim's constitution, and/or an *amissio* rune, which slows blood loss and speeds natural blood replacement.

WARDS

You've probably heard your fellow Shadowhunters talk about the "wards" of your Institute. Wards are, put simply, magical walls. They are the simplest magic we know of, other than glamours. All Shadowhunter wards are pale reflections of the great wards of our world, the protections that largely prevent demons from entering at whim and that are believed to have been put in place by Heaven, long ago, before the measuring of the passage of time. It is these wards that were somehow "thinned" by the combined power of Sammael and Lilith, to allow the Incursion that prompted the creation of the Nephilim. Although these wards still stand, protecting us from a complete invasion, they allow a steady stream of demonkind that shows no sign of slowing and in fact may be increasing.

In the earliest days of the Nephilim, the first Silent Brothers performed rituals all over the world, intending to bolster these wards by adding our own lesser wards to their power. But wards exist at all levels of power, down through the more everyday wards we use to protect our Institutes, to simple wards that might protect a single room or even a single object, such as a locked chest. Today wards can be quite complex, and specific as to who is warded and who is allowed through.

Demonic magic, of course, has its own wards, which work similarly.

—— DEMONIC MAGIC ——

We use the term "demonic magic" to encompass all magic whose origin lies in the Void. This includes the magic employed directly by demons, which is mostly beyond our mortal understanding; the supernatural powers possessed by vampires and werewolves; and the complex but organized magic researched and performed by warlocks.

Demonic magic is by nature chaotic. Whereas the magic of Heaven is given to us whole and complete, the magic of Hell is a slippery, dangerous, growing beast. It is not known what limits might exist on demonic magic, in terms of either what it can do or how powerful its effects can become. There is much that has been discovered, and much knowledge that can be relied upon in dealings with demons (or warlocks), but never forget that—unlike our Marks, which begin and end with the bindings of the Gray Book—the edges of the demon world are full of magic unknown to us.

Shadowhunters are categorically unable to learn demonic magic, or to inscribe or even to read demonic runes. It is as if our knowledge of the Marks of the Gray Book prevents our minds from successfully being able to comprehend the Marks' demonic cousins, however we might study them. Nephilim who are expert at the reading and writing of Marks often say that trying to read demonic runes is like trying to understand someone speaking a language that sounds tantalizingly similar to your own but is too different for you to grasp the meaning.

Different kinds of demonic magic have different weaknesses— ways the magic can be neutralized—but almost all magic can be disrupted with running water. More powerful magic can sometimes overcome this, but on the other hand, larger bodies of running water are more disruptive and require more power to overcome. Thus, many powerful warlocks could successfully perform magic in the presence of a babbling brook, whereas only the most powerful in the world, or the most powerful Greater Demons, could successfully perform magic on the open ocean.

Has the Clave considered fire trucks? Just drive around the world hosing demons down?

Doesn't really work that way. You can't just spray a demon with water like it's a bad cat.

DARK MAGIC VERSUS DEMONIC MAGIC

It is important to understand that all "demonic magic" is not evil, at least not when it is used by creatures other than demons. Warlocks are in their essence human, and therefore have the same free will as all other humans. Vampires and werewolves have a demonic source for their powers but are also human and possess free will. All may choose to use demonic magic for good or for ill.

We use the term "dark magic" to refer to that demonic magic whose purpose or orientation is essentially evil. This would include such things as necromancy, the summoning of demons, the domination of an intelligent mind against its will, and so on. Dark magic is generally outlawed under the Law, although exceptions may be made for dark magic that is performed out of necessity in the course of Shadowhunter business—for example, summoning a demon in order to interrogate it.

Demons, being purely demonic and possessing none of the human about them, are considered to be performing dark magic no matter what they are doing. Technically, manifesting themselves in our world at all under their own will is an act of dark magic and is punishable under the Law.

164

Dark magic may be identified by some of its telltale markers. Its practice leaves behind a lingering aura that can usually be detected by a warlock, and often there is a persistent reek of brimstone and rot that even an untrained Shadowhunter can identify (although it will be typically glamoured away from mundane detection).

DEALING WITH DEMONIC MAGIC

The biggest danger of demonic magic for Shadowhunters is that, because its boundaries are soft and unclear, it can be difficult to understand the parameters of the magic one is dealing with, or what the capabilities of a magic user might be. There is no substitute for experience, of course, but we offer here some thoughts on common demonic magic and basic knowledge that may be useful for the new Shadowhunter.

DIMENSIONAL MAGIC

You will rarely encounter dimensional magic; the ability to perform it is very rare. Demons encourage the idea that they are constantly popping in and out of dimensions on a whim, but in truth none but the most powerful Greater Demons can do this. Demons travel to our dimension not through their own magic but by making use of the holes and worn spots enhanced and highlighted by Sammael a thousand years ago; as far as we know, none of the common demons have the power or knowledge to continue the thinning magic he performed. Some Greater Demons may have the power to teleport themselves to different locations within our dimension, and some may be able to open temporary weak dimensional Portals, but a demon who claims to have power over the spaces between worlds is almost certainly lying to you.

Warlocks who can perform dimensional magic are even rarer, although they do exist and are frequently able to charge exorbitant fees for their services. The most dangerous dimensional magic that warlocks may possess is the ability to create dimensional "pockets"—small spaces between dimensions, where objects or people may be hidden and kept concealed from tracking magic.

NECROMANCY

For as long as there have been warlocks, there have been tales of supposed necromancers, magic users who were capable of returning the dead to life. Do not be fooled by these tales: There is no way for the magic of Hell to return the dead to the world of the living. That is magic that is reserved for Heaven and its servants—not the Nephilim, for we are but the servants of servants, but the denizens of Heaven itself.

Necromantic rituals do exist in some more obscure and forbidden texts of magic; these, variants on the classic mundane folkloric "bell, book, and candle" method of summoning the dead, produce a semblance of life but not a living creature. These revived beings, in theory, can range from a mindless, shambling revenant to a corpse able to repeat its soul's last living words, but in practice such things are rarely, if ever, seen. Necromancy is among the darkest of dark magic. It is punishable by death, but most warlocks are never punished by the Clave, as they almost never survive their attempts.

HELLMIST

Hellmist, or hellsmoke, is a weapon sometimes used by demons, and occasionally by powerful and evil warlocks, to aid their attacks. It is very dangerous for the unprepared Shadowhunter. It is a kind of conjured demonic fog that mutes the effects of magic. Hellsmoke is able to mute both the angelic magic that Shadowhunters use with our Marks and also other demonic magic. Luckily, few kinds of demons can produce it easily, and those that do will make use of it only rarely, since demons are often dependent on demonic magic to grant them power in our world. For instance, a demon with no eyes who needed magic to see their foe would work against themselves in releasing hellmist.

Hellmist becomes much more dangerous when used to cloak a physical attack, but demons rarely engage in even such simple tactical planning. A coordinated attack of that kind would almost without fail suggest the involvement of a Greater Demon or a powerful dark magician. *And . . . what should you do about that?*

When the Codex doesn't give you a thing to do, assume its advice is, "Run!"

CONJURING OBJECTS FROM NOWHERE

This is not possible. Something cannot be created out of nothing. Warlocks who claim to be able to produce new objects from nowhere, or who appear to do so, are in fact merely teleporting the objects from some location known to them. This is still powerful magic and potentially dangerous, and it may well represent a violation of Law. Warlocks, for all their power, may enjoy fooling mundanes and more credulous young Shadowhunters by claiming more abilities than they have. Do not be deceived.

THE SUMMONING OF DEMONS

While the practice of dark magic by warlocks is an unfortunate reminder of the continued threat demons pose to our own home dimension, and is generally forbidden, such magic is permitted in the course of assisting a Shadowhunter investigation—for instance, when a specific demon must be located or interrogated. In those cases generally a friendly warlock is employed; this has become

much more common since the Accords eased the formerly
tense relationship between Nephilim and warlocks. *Read this to Magnus*
The demon-summoning rituals vary somewhat, *he says "ha!"*
depending on the demon and the warlock involved, but
generally speaking they take the following steps:

- A pentagram or similar summoning circle is drawn
  on the surface on which the demon is to be summoned.
- Demonic runes of various kinds are drawn on the
  summoning circle, often at the points of the pentagram
  or by some other design specified in
  warlock magical lore.
- An invocation is made by the warlock.
- Often a sacrifice of blood is demanded, usually
  provided by the warlock performing the ceremony.
  (Beware any warlock who claims that he will need
  your blood to complete his summoning!)
- If possible, a piece of the demon itself, such as a
  tuft of its fur or some scales or a tooth, is put into
  the pentagram. *Mmmm . . . PIECE OF A DEMON.*

At that point, if the warlock is competent, the demon
should be summoned and bound. Be sure to consult the
warlock ahead of time for any time limits, restrictions, or
forbidden words or hand gestures that might be relevant in
that particular summoning. *Wait, how do you get a piece of a
demon to use to summon a demon if you don't already have*

THE PORTAL *a summoned demon to get a piece of demon from?*

New Shadowhunters usually don't have trouble *. . . What?*
understanding how a Portal works. It transports you *That was a real*
instantly from one place to another by means of your *question!*
passing through it. It is usually set up by a warlock (see
below for the reasons why), and it requires no skill to use.
We include it here, however, because the invention of the

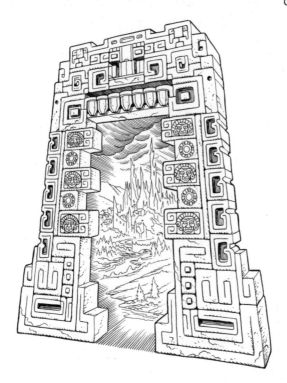

Portal stands as one of the great moments of collaboration between Downworlders and Shadowhunters in the modern age, a powerful demonstration of the creativity and discovery that the Accords can make possible. This invention also represents one of the rare occasions when the Nephilim have been able to advance the knowledge of magic in the human world, despite our pious devotion to the boundaries marked out by the Gray Book.

Today Shadowhunters depend heavily on Portals as a *Oh no it's another history lesson secretly* means for rapid travel all over the world. It would be easy to conclude from this that the Portal is an old and well-established Nephilim tool, but in truth it is a modern invention, dating back to the period between the First and Second Accords. The first successful Portal was created in 1878, a collaboration between Henry Branwell, then head of

169

the London Institute, and a warlock whose name history, unfortunately, does not record. Branwell was at the time only the most recent in a long string of Shadowhunters (mostly Silent Brothers) and warlocks to seek a reliable, safe means of instantaneous travel. Dimensional magic of course has been in existence for as long as there has been magic in our world; the means by which demons are able to slip from their own world to ours is itself magic in the same family as the Portal. There were two major requirements in creating a workable Portal for Shadowhunter use—keeping it stable and safely open for the necessary amount of time and safely closed when no longer needed, and accurately controlling the destination that a Portal would open onto.

Working on his own, Branwell had designed a Portal that had solved the first of these problems; it could be opened and closed, but he could find no way to direct its destination, and so it could not be tested. A Portal opened to an arbitrary location could send a hapless Shadowhunter to any location in our world, to a different world entirely, even to the Void.

The difficulty here turns out to lie in our restriction to Gray Book Marks. We cannot arbitrarily describe a destination using the runic language we are permitted to use. The solution was discovered by Branwell and his anonymous warlock collaborator, and it is an ingenious merging of two runic systems and the magic inherent in the mind of the one traveling through the Portal. First, a "frame" of Marks (which have analogues in both seraphic and demonic runic systems) is created, and inscribed within and around this frame is a set of demonic runes that are drawn in an unstable, unfinished state.

These runes, however, only specify the destination

in vague terms. To "tune" the Portal to the exact location desired, the user of the Portal must picture clearly in their mind the destination they are traveling to. The Portal detects these details and modifies the demonic destination runes on the fly, to exactly describe the far end of the Portal.

This kind of runic manipulation isn't available to Shadowhunters, and so to this day Portals must be created by warlocks. To get around this, a large number of permanent Portals have been established to transport Nephilim to and from Idris, for instance, without having to hire warlocks for every trip. Even so, today Portal construction makes up the vast majority of jobs for warlocks hired by Shadowhunters.

Originally Portals had to be closed manually by their creator once they were no longer needed, but in recent years warlocks have been able to create Portals that close automatically after a certain amount of time has passed. This kind of Portal is what is usually used today, for purposes of safety.

But none of this is relevant to you because you can make new runes, so you can make Portals yourself. Without bothering a warlock.

I know how much those warlocks hate to be bothered.

Did you know you're related to Henry Branwell, at least by marriage? He was married to a Fairchild.

I did not know that. It is sort of weird that you do know that.

I had to memorize a lot of Shadowhunter genealogies at one point.

I can't believe Simon hasn't said anything terrible here yet.

His absence is almost eerie.

DISCUSSION QUESTIONS AND THINGS TO TRY

1. Learn a new rune you haven't ever used before. Practice it here on the page and try applying it in the field.

   I draw enough runes, thanks. Here is a drawing of Chairman Meow instead.

   1A. WHO IS A WOOBUMS? IS IT CHAIRMAN MEOW? IS IT? *Yes it is!* THAT IS CORRECT

2. If possible, witness some (safe and legal!) demonic magic being performed near your home Institute. Discuss with your fellow local Shadowhunters. What magic is taking place in your part of the world?

   It's New York, so . . . all magic? Is there anything we don't have? I'm pretty sure we've got all of it.

3. It can be very useful to learn to make your own magical wards. Find instructions and place a ward on something small, like a jewelry box. Practice removing and resetting the ward, then move on to something a little more complex. And so on.

   Do not do this. Seriously, wards are a big pain. And you almost never have to make your own unless you're replacing a broken one. No one reading the Codex as a new Shadowhunter should jump into making wards. They'll end up warding their own foot or something.

   Note to self: Do not ward own foot. Check.

CHAPTER SEVEN

"SED LEX, DURA LEX"

"THE LAW IS HARD, BUT IT IS THE LAW."

You have been immersed, quickly, in a whole world that is still beyond your reckoning. You've learned not just that there are intelligent magical creatures on Earth who are not purely human, but that there are many of them, and many who wear a human face. These people wield powerful magic and engage in powerful, sometimes violent feuds. You know of the Shadow World and what you will find there. Now we take up the question of how you should act there. *In the most pompous way possible.*

We Nephilim are, primarily in the Shadow World, the keepers of peace, and thus the keepers of the Law. The Law—our Covenant with Raziel—tells us what does and does not fall under our jurisdiction, how we may punish violations of the Law, and what rules we ourselves must obey in our interactions with mundanes, with Downworlders, and with one another.

The Law of the Nephilim is not a full code of conduct for Shadowhunters in all realms of their lives. First and foremost comes the injunction attributed to Jonathan Shadowhunter himself: "You are Man; serve Man; live among Man." Though Idris may come with its own body of general laws, the Shadowhunters assigned all over the world are expected to live among the basic moral codes of their civilization. Our own Law is foremost in importance, but mundane law must be observed as well. *Really? The Covenant says that? Note: Ask Jace.*

Yes we are supposed to follow mundane laws.

. . . Really?

Some of us are more careful than others.

175

HOW THE LAW AFFECTS: YOU

- You must investigate **any known instances** of Covenant Law being **violated**. In fact, you are required to consider even **rumors**, **urban legends**, and **folktales**, to assess their credibility.
- You **cannot reveal the Shadow World** to mundanes. In fact, Raziel's guidance is that as we protect and save mundanes they must not know they are being saved.

What about mundane governments?

- Whenever possible, you must **obey the mundane laws** in the place where you live. *"Whenever possible," nudge nudge*

Mundanes who already know are ok

but . . . ?

- You must **never commit a crime against another Shadowhunter**. These violations are punished much more harshly by the Clave than crimes against mundanes or Downworlders. This is not because of moral superiority, or because a Shadowhunter is a more valuable person than a non-Shadowhunter, but rather because we Nephilim are few and our lives short. To cause another Shadowhunter to come to harm is to benefit the demons who seek to destroy us.

I am shocked!
Shocked!
Oh, stop.
See?!

- **Collaboration or collusion** with the demons who seek to destroy us **is considered treason** and is usually a capital crime. Colluding with demons to bring direct harm to Shadowhunters would bring down the Clave's harshest possible punishment, the end of that family's existence among the Nephilim. The perpetrator's Marks would be stripped and he would be made Forsaken, left to go insane and die. The rest of his family would merely have their Marks removed and be made mundane, removed from our ranks entirely.

Okay okay fine.

176

Do a lot of new Shadowhunters need to be warned not to collude with demons and not to kill each other?

I guess the Clave wants you to know they mean business.

HOW THE LAW AFFECTS: DOWNWORLDERS

Since the Accords, Downworlders have been subject to the Law of the Covenant, with their consent. Downworlders are meant to police themselves, with Shadowhunters interfering only in cases where problems are too severe, or where issues affect other parts of Downworld or the mundane world. Downworlders also have the right to conduct their internal business privately, without the interference or oversight of the Nephilim. For instance, we allow werewolves to fight to the death for control of their packs. We cannot protect these werewolves from possible interference from mundane law enforcement, but we also don't consider these deaths to be murder under the Law.

A special exception here is the case of dark magic (see the Grimoire, Chapter 6). The practice of dark magic—necromancy, demon-summoning, magical torture, and so on—is strictly forbidden, and neither warlocks nor faeries are permitted to practice it. Exceptions are sometimes made for specific rituals done as part of a Shadowhunter investigation, but they are very rare.

REPARATIONS

Downworlders have the right under the Law to appeal to the Clave if they believe they have been mistreated by Shadowhunters, or believe that Shadowhunters have broken the Law in their dealings with them. They may request Reparations, monetary compensation for the harm brought to them. They may also call a trial, which will be administered by representatives of the Clave, and Reparations will be paid if the Downworlder can prove their case.

Mundanes also have the right to petition for Reparations, but obviously this comes up infrequently; only a few cases have been seen of mundane Reparations in the entire history of the Nephilim.

The Accords greatly improved the rights of Downworlders under the Law, and so the nature of Reparations changed significantly. Prior to the Accords, Downworlders had essentially no recourse or specific protection under Shadowhunter law; a Shadowhunter could kill a Downworlder under only the suspicion of wrongdoing, and all that could be done would be for a next of kin to file for Reparations. In the last hundred years claims for Reparations have decreased, now that Nephilim can be held legally responsible for abusing Downworlders whether or not someone comes forth to demand Reparations.

SPOILS

The term "spoils" refers to the taking of the possessions and wealth of a Downworlder as part of the punishment for a crime. Typically these spoils are forfeited to the Shadowhunter who has been wronged by the Downworlder. Or the spoils are forfeited to the Clave's treasury if no specific Shadowhunter seems the proper recipient. In practice, however, Downworlders' spoils have almost always ended up in the hands of individual Shadowhunter families. In fact, for many old wealthy Shadowhunter families, a goodly portion of their prosperity originates in spoils granted by the Clave.

The practice of taking spoils probably began very early in Nephilim history, but in isolated and informal ways. Spoils are first mentioned in official Clave Law around 1400, but records indicate that the Clave had been officially granting spoils in trials for years already. The awarding of spoils was no more or less popular than other forms of punishment, until the Hunts and the Schism of the sixteenth and seventeenth centuries made the awarding of spoils the most common punishment doled out by the Clave. There were two reasons for this. The first was to legitimize and place some limits on the pillaging of Downworlder property

178

that was happening regardless of Clave involvement; the second, which may seem counterintuitive, was to save Downworlders' lives. In the existing frenzy of Downworlder persecution, which could easily have involved widespread murder, it was hoped that the promise of spoils would stay the Shadowhunters' weapons in favor of the larger benefit to them of spoils. *See, we had to steal their stuff to help them.*

The practice of granting spoils lost some of its popularity with the end of the Hunts, but it was still the most common punishment for Downworlder offenses until the First Accords. For all of the language of philosophy and Law thrown about, much of the Shadowhunter opposition to the First Accords came down to economics. Those families strongly dependent on spoils for their wealth stood to lose quite a lot. They argued that the rules restricting spoils would harm the Clave directly. Although spoils were not technically taxed, it was considered virtuous for Shadowhunters, especially the wealthier families, to tithe a percentage of them to the Clave. The First Accords created the beginnings of complex legal language that did not eliminate spoils but strongly restricted the severity of the punishment, and also provided that the punishment of taking spoils from Downworlders could be executed only as part of an official sentence at a trial performed by the Clave. Many spoils have been returned in the past hundred years. Although, in cases where the family of the original owner could not be located, many other spoils have been placed on display in various Institutes, as historical curiosities.

Nice motorcycle, by the way, Jace.

That's not spoils. That was illegal. I was impounding it.

HOW THE LAW AFFECTS: MUNDANES

Mom suggested that I talk to Luke about spoils. I did.
He went off on a lecture again. Here are the notes.

Mundanes are not subject to Covenant Law. They are not signers of the Accords, and only a few in the world know of the existence of Shadowhunters or the Shadow World. Even mundane members

Luke says:
No limits on spoils during werewolf hunts. All that in the Codex ridiculous; just made pillaging nice and legal.
• Returned some spoils after Accords, but not much—couldn't find families.
• Didn't even try to return money taken. That would be impossible.
• Apparently in Germany there's an Institute that was taken as a spoil from some vampires. They're still fighting about it.

179

of demonic cults cannot be prosecuted under the Law, since they are meddling with forces beyond their ken. (**Tip!** Demonic cults can be most easily neutralized by going after the demon being worshipped, who *can* be prosecuted and indeed killed under the Law.) *Well, thank goodness.*

This is one of the most controversial parts of the Law. Every Accords proceeding has featured strident demands from both Shadowhunters and Downworlders that mundanes be held accountable for their behavior. These demands are always declined, for the simple reason that our charge to keep our world hidden from mundanes must be paramount.

THE INQUISITOR

The Inquisitor is the Shadowhunter responsible for investigating breaches of the Law by Nephilim. Not even the Consul can refuse to cooperate with her investigations. When Nephilim are put on trial before the Council, the Inquisitor typically serves as the prosecuting attorney, and recommends or requests specific sentences for guilty parties. (These recommendations must then be ratified by the Council.)

The Inquisitor stands outside the rest of Shadowhunter government of Clave and Council. She is typically disliked by the Nephilim at large, because of the authority she wields. It is an infamously thankless job. But our history is full of the stories of heroic Inquisitors who have kept our society from falling into corruption, by rooting out Lawbreakers and seeing that they are punished.

2002 ADDENDUM

The Inquisitor's most recent high-profile task was the investigation of the Circle, Valentine Morgenstern's band of dissident Shadowhunters, after the failure of his Uprising against the Clave. The Inquisitor had to perform a complex task of separating out those who had been made to follow Morgenstern, those who had done so of their own free will, those who had recanted his beliefs but had been unable to leave out of fear for their lives, those who still believed in his apocalyptic vision, and so on. Most Circle members' lives were spared, and the punishments of the guilty varied widely, from compulsory tithes, to incarceration, to the loss of administrative duties, to exile from Idris. Thus is the Inquisitor's job a difficult one, and her role in meting out justice complex and imperfect.

—— THE LIFE OF A SHADOWHUNTER ——

Though Shadowhunters come from all corners of our world, we are Shadowhunters first, and citizens of our own ancestral homelands second. In the thousand years that we have existed, we have lived apart from mundanes, and the life of a Shadowhunter includes many features unique to us and our history. These are outlined here so that they may be recognized, and so that you may behave appropriately at times of celebration, struggle, and grief. *I had a book like this section for Judaism when I was little.*

BIRTH

The birth of a new Shadowhunter is an occasion for great celebration. We are not a numerous people, and we tend to die young; therefore any new young Shadowhunter is a cause for joy and delight. Births are normally presided over by Silent Brothers, who are able to use both their Marks and their knowledge of medicine to keep mother and child safe and healthy. As a result, we have always enjoyed a much higher rate of survival and healthiness in births than the mundane population.

When a Shadowhunter is born, it is traditional for a number of protective spells to be placed on the infant by an Iron Sister and a Silent Brother, representatives of their orders. (Usually the Silent Brother is the same person to have presided over the birth.) These are meant to strengthen the child, both physically and spiritually, in preparation for her first Marks later in life, and also to protect her from demonic influence and possession.

Note: ask Mom about this, me?!

TRAINING

Most new Shadowhunters want to know where they, or their children, will go to school. There is no such thing as a Shadow-hunter school in the way mundanes use the term. Instead young Nephilim are tutored, either in their family homes or in small groups at their local Institutes. The training of new Shadowhunters is one of the responsibilities of all adult Shadowhunters, who are meant to share teaching duties, each from his own expertise. Parents are meant to lead the project of training their own children; orphaned Shadowhunters under the age of eighteen are the responsibility of the Clave, and will usually be sent to be raised and trained in their local Institute.

Shadowhunters (other than Silent Brothers) do not typically do scholarly work when young. What mundanes would think of as "higher education" is the kind of learning that we do in our older years, when we are no longer able to fight effectively or safely and we turn our minds to intensive, focused research and study.

MEN AND WOMEN IN TRAINING

Male and female Shadowhunter children receive identical training today, and are expected to reach the same standard of achievement in their educations. It has always been true that the Nephilim have included both men and women, but it is only recently that all women have been given full training as warriors. There have always been women warriors among us, but prior to 150 years ago or so, they were quite rare. Women were mostly, prior to that, keepers of Institutes, teachers, healers, and the like. Although the Laws officially preventing most women from becoming full Shadowhunter fighters were revoked in the mid-nineteenth century, it wasn't until the mid-twentieth century that Clave women were given combat training as a matter of course from childhood, as Clave men always had been.

The women warriors of Nephilim past took Boadicea, the great warrior who led her people in revolt against imperial Rome, as their patron and model, and that tradition has continued to this day. *Wooooo ladies rule*

YOUR FIRST MARK

Most Shadowhunters get their first Marks at twelve years of age. Since you, the reader, are likely to have entered the Nephilim from the mundane world, rather than being born into a Nephilim family, you may well be significantly older. This carries with it some inherent risks. It is usually considered ideal to get your first Marks when you are no younger than twelve, and no older than twenty, though there are exceptions. The older the person receiving the Mark, the greater the chance of a bad reaction.

Some things to keep in mind when receiving your first Mark:

- If there is going to be a problem, it is not going to happen immediately. If you react poorly to the influx of angelic power, Shadowhunters will be standing by ready to cut the skin, which will disrupt the Mark and stop the effect short. You'll then receive full medical and magical attention.

· The act of inscribing Marks on skin creates a sensation that most describe as like an "icy burn." This sensation will fade with time as your body grows accustomed to being Marked. The inscription of Marks also creates a scent in the air of something faintly burned. This scent will *not* fade with time. Do not be alarmed.

· Sometimes the newly Marked go into shock. The good news is, if this happens to you, you are unlikely to notice, because you will be in shock. Shadowhunters are trained to recognize shock along with other bad reactions to Marks and will treat you accordingly.

· In the next few days, especially if you are at high risk for side effects, you may experience such symptoms as screaming nightmares, night terrors, fear-driven bed-wetting, stark perceptions of the bottomless abyss of existence, restless arm syndrome, apocalyptic visions, acute illusory stigmata, and/or the ability to temporarily speak with animals. These reactions are normal and only temporary. *"acute illusory stigmata?"* Barely ever happens. I thi

· If you are not absolutely sure that you are not a warlock, we implore you to be tested before being Marked. Families with the vagaries of faerie blood, or even with known werewolves in the lineage, should be fine, since the Nephilim power will overwhelm these.

So this is more a "do as the Codex says, not as Jace does" situation, I gue

AFTER YOUR FIRST MARK Since he just Marks any girl he likes. apparently. When she is dying, yes

Congratulations! You have survived your first Mark. We can promise that each successive Mark is easier than the previous. Your eagerness to learn by returning to the Codex is commendable, but

184

before you return to your studies, you should make sure that the Shadowhunter inscribing you confirms you are capable of work. You may find a need to sleep extensively; this too is normal.

The Codex sure does congratulate you a lot.

GAINING THE SIGHT

Congratulations!
Don't second-guess this decision!

Unless you are among those rare mundanes born with the Sight (see the Grimoire for details), you will need to learn to see through glamours. You may have started this process already. Usually, new adult Shadowhunters first receive a Voyance Mark, and several other temporary Marks that enhance magical vision. (We do not keep these Marks, because in the long term they impair normal vision.) You will then be shown glamours of various kinds and will be trained in seeing through them.

"BLIND" NEPHILIM

Most Shadowhunters have the Sight from birth, and those who do not mostly gain it in the first two or three years of life. Some, however, are born "blind" and must be trained to see. Usually it is sufficient to deliberately show children glamours and their revealed true shapes; this produces full Sight in almost all Shadowhunter children by the time they are beginning their training in earnest, at five or six years of age. It is only as humans grow older that we need the assistance of Marks to initially develop the skill.

How could I possibly have already known this, Codex?

Did you know?

Before it was made illegal, it was traditional in some parts of the world to "jump-start" a Nephilim child's Sight by inscribing a deliberately weak Voyance Mark on the child, at a much younger age than we would today consider safe. (In some cultures the Mark was inscribed and then the skin under it was purposefully wounded to disrupt its effectiveness.) When the Marking was successful, some haphazard level of Sight occurred at times for the child, and at least sometimes this successfully caused the child to have the Sight permanently even after the Mark was removed. Unfortunately, this process also occasionally caused children to die of shock, from the simultaneous effect of a too-early Mark and the abrupt appearance of Sight. The practice is still done in a few places, but thankfully it has mostly disappeared in the modern age.

MARRIAGE

If you are already married, your spouse is very likely also becoming a Shadowhunter alongside you. If you are not married, when you someday do marry, you will do so as a Shadowhunter. Marriage is considered one of the sacred tasks of the Nephilim, both because the union strengthens the community and because it brings about more Nephilim.

Many hundreds of years ago aristocratic Shadowhunter families typically arranged marriages for their children in order to strengthen and mix family lines; in the modern age this practice is mostly extinct, and Shadowhunters choose their partners based on their own feelings of love and affection, as most mundane cultures today do.

Shadowhunters have always exchanged trinkets and tokens to mark marriages, to signify love and connection between the bride and the groom, mostly borrowing these customs from their cultures of origin or their current cultures. Among Nephilim, marriage is consecrated officially by the exchange of Marks. On each participant a Mark is placed on the arm, and another over the heart. This tradition is believed to come from the Hebrew Bible, whose Song of Solomon reads:

Set me as a seal upon thine heart, as a seal upon thine arm: for love is strong as death; jealousy is cruel as the grave.

INTERMARRIAGE

Shadowhunters are permitted to marry other Shadowhunters and, in most cases, Downworlders. (Since the Clave's primary concern is the ability to birth more Shadowhunters, it is somewhat frowned upon to marry a warlock or a vampire, since they will have no children, but it is allowed.) Shadowhunters are *not* permitted to marry mundanes. They are, however, allowed to petition the Clave and ask that the mundane they wish to marry be allowed to become a Shadowhunter, in a process known as Ascension. (You may even be reading this Codex because you are yourself an Ascender!)

The Shadowhunter who wishes to marry a mundane applies for Ascension on behalf of his partner. For three months the Clave considers the petition, examining the history of the Shadowhunter who has applied, and his family, in addition to the background and nature of the possible Ascender. Of necessity this is all done without the knowledge of the Ascender; prior to the Clave's decision in the affirmative, it remains illegal to tell the mundane applicant any details of the ways of the Nephilim. Once the Clave has granted the petition, the Ascender is told about her situation, and she embarks on three months' study of Shadowhunter Law and culture. At the end of these three months, the Ascender is given to drink from the Mortal Cup and made a Nephilim; provided she survives this process, she is rendered a full Shadowhunter, with all the protections and rights of the Law that any Shadowhunter would have. *"provided she survives"?!*

187

ASCENSION OF CHILDREN

Though it is very rare, Shadowhunters in the position of adopting a mundane child may petition the Clave for the Ascension of that child. In almost all cases this Ascension is granted, especially inasmuch as the child is entering an existing Shadowhunter family and will take an existing Shadowhunter family name. The three-month waiting period still applies, but after Ascension the child is typically brought up and educated in the way of any other young Shadowhunter.

What about same-sex marriage?

A BRIEF HISTORY OF SHADOWHUNTER INTERMARRIAGE

Okay, I went and asked Jace about it, because he is cruel and heartless. Actually, for me to research in the library. I think he didn't know the answer and was covering it up.

In the earliest days of the Nephilim, our highest priority was recruitment. Marrying mundanes was not only legal, it was encouraged. Shadowhunters were taught to view their search for a spouse as a kind of recruitment, and Shadowhunter families boasted about the quality of mundanes they had brought into the Nephilim by their children's marriages.

The practice grew much less common as the population of Shadowhunters became fairly stable and recruitment became a lower priority. In the 1400s the Council officially revoked Institute heads' ability to create new Shadow-hunters without Clave approval. The Clave representatives in Idris had no mechanism for evaluating a possible marriage, and began refusing almost all requests for inter-marriages with mundanes. In 1599 the Council outlawed all Shadowhunter-mundane intermarriages of any kind.

One would expect outrage from Shadowhunter families, but in fact the new Law appeared during the height of the Schism and the Hunts (see Appendix A). These events made

Your service as a Shadowhunter will never depend on knowing how intermarriage worked five hundred years ago. I promise.

This sidebar is very long and is full of dates. It can be safely ignored.

188

Answer: Same-sex marriage recognized in Idris, legal for Shadowhunters in countries where it is allowed. There has never been an Ascension of same-sex partners, but Ascension very rare now so could happen in future anytime.

the Shadowhunters a much more isolated, militaristic, and monastic organization for a time. Nephilim stopped living among mundanes, as they had done in European villages for hundreds of years, and reorganized their Institutes as barracks. Even after the end of the Schism, this isolationism remained for many generations. To some extent the principles of isolation established in the Schism still guide the relationship of the Nephilim with mundanes today.

The fact of the modern world, however, is that Nephilim, especially in large cities and other populous areas, cannot help but encounter mundanes in their day-to-day lives, and no one today would consider it reasonable to forbid Shadowhunters to interact with mundanes at all. Thus in 1804 the Law prohibiting intermarriage was revoked and the method of Ascension developed. Ascension has always been, and remains, rare, but it is a crucial tool for keeping Shadowhunter populations thriving, happy, and dynamic.

BATTLE

There are many seasons of a Shadowhunter's life, and many turns that life may take, but the core occupation of the Shadowhunter is, so to speak, the hunting of shadows. We are warriors, holy soldiers in a ceaseless battle, and while our adult lives include the same joys and sorrows as any mundane's, the defining characteristic of our lives is that of fighting, of seeking demons invading our world and sending them, broken, back to theirs. It is the greatest honor for a Nephilim to die in combat with demons. Thus we say: Do not shirk from battle. Have faith, seek courage. A Shadowhunter who does not fight is not a complete

Shadowhunter. (Unless that Shadowhunter is a Silent Brother or Iron Sister, of course.)

It is true, however, that many Shadowhunters put aside their weapons as they grow older, and seek a quieter life of study or research. But we do not do this until we have lived a full warrior's life and are ready to put it aside with a feeling of completion.

Did You Know?

It is considered bad luck to say "good-bye" or "good luck" to a Shadowhunter who is going off to battle. One must behave with confidence, as though victory is assured and return is certain, not a matter of chance. *I actually did know that!*

Even I knew that. Come on, Codex.

THOSE WHO LEAVE *Everyone knows THAT. Why do I keep letting*

Rarely, a Shadowhunter will choose to leave the Clave and *you write in th* enter the mundane world. There may be many reasons *thing?* for this, but the Nephilim do not often look kindly on those who choose this path, whatever their reason. We are too few as it is, and we are meant to regard our status as Nephilim as a gift from Heaven and a divine calling, not as an accident of birth or a career path to be chosen or declined.

As such the Law is clear on the responsibilities of those who leave the Clave:

- They must sever all contact with Shadowhunters, even those of their own family who remain in the Clave. They must never so much as speak to Nephilim or be spoken to by them.

- In renouncing the Clave they also renounce the Clave's obligation to offer them assistance in case of danger. They are not even afforded the protections given by Law to mundanes.

- Their children, even future children, remain Shadowhunters by blood and may be claimed by the Clave. Shadowhunter blood breeds true, and the children of Shadowhunters will be Shadowhunters, even if their parents have left, even if their Marks have been stripped.
- Every six years a representative of the Clave is sent to ask those children of ex-Shadowhunters if the children would like to leave their family and be raised among Shadowhunters in an Institute, as if they were orphans. Only when the child has turned eighteen does this practice end. (Those who reject the Nephilim into adulthood are not treated with the stigma of ex-Shadowhunters but have the same rights of protection as any mundane. The Clave has no wish to punish children for the crimes of their parents.)
- A Shadowhunter who has been turned into a Downworlder can no longer be Nephilim but should not be punished in the manner of those who chose to leave. In these cases the person gives up the protection owed him by the Clave for being a Shadowhunter but becomes newly entitled to the protection granted to Downworlders.

DEATH

Most Shadowhunters die as Shadowhunters. And most die in battle with demons. Major buzzkill, Codex.

We Nephilim burn our dead, discarding the fragile physical body that has trapped us and restricted us for our short human lives. Our remains are then interred. Those who die in Idris are

191

traditionally entombed in its necropolis, outside Alicante's walls. Those who die outside Idris are entombed in the Silent City. The Silent Brothers have responsibility over the dead in both locations. Most Shadowhunter families are old families and as a result have not merely grave plots but large family tombs and mausoleums, often one in each of the two necropolises.

Before being set on the funeral pyre, the Shadowhunter's body is presented so that words of mourning can be spoken and those left behind can pay their last respects. Those in mourning traditionally wear white, and Mark themselves in red. The eyes of the dead Shadowhunter are bound with white silk, and he is laid to rest with his arms crossed over his chest, a seraph blade clutched in the right hand and resting over his heart. Funeral rites vary depending on the part of the world the Shadowhunter is from but traditionally conclude with a sentence from *The Odes of Horace*: *Pulvis et umbra sumus*. "We are dust and shadows."

Hoo boy, I can't read this right now. No no no. Too much.

Yeah, for me too. We've had a little too much dust and shadows lately.

——— SILENT BROTHERS ———
AND IRON SISTERS

THE SILENT BROTHERS

Our Unnerving Allies

And Jonathan took his stele, the first stele, and slowly he drew a V, then another, then another, in a continuous line, VVVVV, from David's upper lip to his bottom lip and back again. The stele was warm in his hand and left a fine indentation of crosshatch that remained even after the stele's point was withdrawn.

Jonathan drew back, finished, and cocked his head at David, not sure if the Mark had taken.

David began to open his mouth to speak, and as he did, the lines on his mouth burned gold, and his lips caught just slightly open, held together by black threads, thin but strong. Jonathan stepped back and lifted the stele without thought, unsure. But the corners of David's mouth turned up slightly in what he was now able to produce in lieu of a smile.

"Sir?" Jonathan said, his voice wavering.

It is good, Shadowhunter, David said abruptly in Jonathan's mind. His voice was strong and calm and echoed in Jonathan's head much more loudly than Jonathan would have expected. *Now,* David went on, lifting two fingers to his own face like a gesture of blessing. *Now the eyes.*

—From *Jonathan and David in Idris,* by Arnold
 Featherstone, 1970

193

The Silent Brothers are indeed our brothers—brothers to all Nephilim. Do not be frightened of them. Their appearance may be ~No suddo~ ~moves,~ disconcerting, or even sickening, to you on first glance, but they ~though.~ are Nephilim, like you, and you fight on the same side, toward the same goals. (Most Shadowhunters get over their fear of Silent Brothers the first time they are injured in battle and the Brothers nurse them back to health.) It is worth noting that many Silent Brothers enjoy unsettling their fellow Nephilim, and deliberately play up their spookier features. This is a kind of hazing and should be taken as the good fun it is intended to be.

It is easy for new Nephilim to look upon the Silent Brothers as somehow more holy or angelic or powerful than the rest of us, but this is not in fact the case. The Silent Brothers rarely fight and lack any of the many combat runes that you will likely receive to enhance your physical and mental abilities. Instead they have taken Marks upon themselves that grant them access to the more esoteric corners of the Gray Book. They are our doctors, our scholars, our archivists. To them is given jurisdiction over the Nephilim dead. This of course includes those who rest in the Silent City, but the cemetery of Idris, too, is the Silent Brothers' domain.

The Marks that the Silent Brothers use in their work are not so much forbidden to other Nephilim as hidden from our sight. In essence, parts of the Gray Book are locked and invisible to us, and the Marks the Brothers are inscribed with are the key. The Silent Brothers therefore have access to strange magic that you will not see performed by other Nephilim. In exchange for their special abilities, they have given up some of their humanity, moving farther from the Earth and closer to Heaven than the rest of us. They are still human, but their extraordinary nature makes them often disconcerting to us: They leave no footprints, do not cast shadows, do not move their mouths to speak, and do not sleep.

194

Their bodies are tugged upward by Heaven, just as vampires' bodies are tugged downward by Hell.

Befitting their seraphic alliance, the Silent Brothers are sometimes called the Grigori. The term refers to the Watchers, one of the higher orders of angels (the Watchers are the angels who are present in the trial of Nebuchadnezzar in the Hebrew Bible, for example), and is applied to the Silent Brothers not to claim their status as more heavenly than other Nephilim, but rather as a reference to their role among the Shadowhunters: watchers rather than fighters. The term has gone out of fashion and is considered archaic but can be found in many older Nephilim writings.

The official habit of the Silent Brothers is a parchment-colored, hooded robe, belted at the waist. Novice Silent Brothers will usually have plain robes, while those who have advanced to full Brotherhood will have decorative Marks circling the cuffs and hems of their robes, in bloodred ink. High-ranking Brothers are sometimes known to carry scepters; these scepters are usually pure silver and are also decorated with Marks, with the head carved in a figurative symbolic shape, such as an angel with outstretched wings, a chalice, or the hilt of a sword. Silent Brothers cast no shadows on the rare occasions they are found in the sun; this is widely believed to be an affectation, like the robe, rather than having some actual purpose.

The Silent Brothers must, by Law, have both their eyes and mouths shut with Marks. There are several different Marks that accomplish this, and the different processes vary, from magically stitching the eyes and mouth shut; to merely keeping the eyes and mouth permanently closed with the Mark of Fettering; to cleanly removing the eyes and/or mouth entirely, leaving blank spaces of flesh where they once were. The latter is, obviously, the most permanent and irreversible of these and is considered the most devout means of Marking oneself as a Silent Brother.

THE IRON SISTERS

The Iron Sisters are a monastic order, like the Silent Brothers, the members of which have taken Marks upon themselves for a specific purpose that requires them to become more than merely human. In the case of the Sisters, however, they have taken upon themselves the ability to work the angelic stone *adamas*, and craft it and whatever other mundane materials are needed into the arms, armor, and tools that keep the Nephilim alive and protected. The Sisters are the only Nephilim permitted to handle *adamas pur*, unworked *adamas*.

Like the Brothers, the Iron Sisters must join the order by taking Marks upon themselves that act as keys to unlocking normally hidden sections of the Gray Book. These Marks also serve to distance them from the rest of humanity. (The Marks are different between the two orders, and being Marked as a Silent Brother does not give you access to the Iron Sisters' Marks, nor vice versa.) Also like the Silent Brothers, the Iron Sisters are not fighters, do not marry, and do not normally attend Council meetings or venture outside of their usual domain.

Iron Sisters are rarely encountered by most Nephilim, but when they are, they are significantly less unsettling in appearance than the Silent Brothers. Their eyes and mouths are not magically closed, and they can neither read minds nor speak telepathically. They wear simple clothes, long white gowns bound tightly at the wrists and waist by demon-wire, to protect their clothes from the holy fires in which their materials are worked. Apart from an appearance of agelessness, their only odd physical feature is their eyes, which typically glow with the colors of flames. It is said that the fires of their great forges burn behind their eyes.

Despite their somewhat more familiar mien, the Iron Sisters are even more private and removed from Nephilim society than the Silent Brothers. They live in solitude in their great Adamant Citadel—whose location on the Earth is unknown to any other Nephilim—and rarely venture outside their fortress. They do not like to be bothered and prefer to work in isolation. A Shadowhunter may live many years without seeing even one Iron Sister in the flesh.

The first Iron Sister, Abigail Shadowhunter, was concerned that despite the gender neutrality of the Shadowhunters, the Sisters would need to be protected from unwanted interference from male Shadowhunters, and so the Adamant Citadel was built to be, and has always been, open only to female Shadowhunters. Indeed, only women are permitted to speak to Iron Sisters.

DISCUSSION QUESTIONS AND THINGS TO TRY

1. Why do you think the Nephilim live under such a strict
    code of Law? How does it benefit our overall mission?

    Sheer unbridled cussedness. Being the baddest hombres in town.

    I wouldn't have put it that way, but that's pretty much the answer
    the Codex is looking for.

    Law and order good! Chaos and anarchy bad!
    Chaos and anarchy also part of our tools, but the Codex doesn't like
    to admit it.

2. Have you been Marked? Describe the experience here.
    Did you have a bad reaction to it? Did you notice it
    working immediately? How have any Marks since the
    first Mark felt different?

    The Codex actually sounds kind of creepy here.
    "Yeeees, tell me eeeeverything." I was Marked by a
    very cute boy with terrible impulse control. I don't
    remember because I was basically unconscious but
    everyone was mad at him when I woke up. The end.
    love Clary.

    Oh my God, your love is so epic.

198

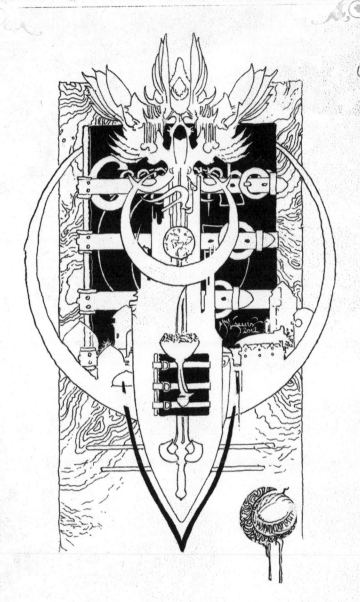

CHAPTER EIGHT

GEOGRAPHIE

IDRIS, THE NEPHILIM HOMELAND

Idris is our country, our land of sanctuary and safety. If you, soon-to-be Shadowhunter, have not yet traveled there, you will likely do so in order to drink from the Cup and receive your first Marks, and there you will see the beauty and tranquility that have made it the best-loved of all Shadowhunter places. Angelic enchantment appears in each leaf, each river stone, each dwelling. The land stands presided over by the soaring fingers of *adamas* that form the towers protecting its capital, Alicante. These towers surround us with angelic light and shield the city and its people from demonkind. Usually.

WHERE IS IDRIS? WHAT IS IT LIKE?

The country of Idris is small, barely visible on a map of Europe. It is in fact little more than the city of Alicante, the plains that gently unroll beneath its walls, and the surrounding mountain range that protects it. Alicante is the only city—indeed, the only major settled area—in the country. This makes much of Idris difficult to traverse, even for Shadowhunters; its mountains are impassable except in high summer, due to heavy snows, and its woods, especially Brocelind Forest, are dense and unmarked by trails. Idris is, nonetheless, very beautiful country: low Alpine, stacked with sheaves of pine trees, among which meander countless rivulets and brooks. Though the land is different from any of its mundane neighbors—Germany, France, Switzerland—it evokes the same beauty as the landscapes of those countries.

Idris was not, as is commonly believed, made from land "stolen" from its bordering countries. Instead Raziel created an entirely new country, like blowing a bubble, in the middle of Europe. It is land made for no purpose other than to be a home for the Nephilim.

HOW TO GET TO IDRIS

Practice, practice, practice.

In order to reach Idris by air, one must fly to one of the airports in a neighboring country and travel overland across its border. Those who are used to the delights of mundane transportation technology may find this somewhat retrogressive, but we invite you to think of it instead as charmingly quaint. Of course, until the beginning of the twentieth century, the only means of reaching Idris at all was overland travel. The travel problem caused by Idris's landlocked status was eventually solved by the invention of the Portal, now the most common means of getting there and back.

THE WARDS OF IDRIS

Come visit the wards! You can't see them!

The wards around Idris are unique, and have proved impossible to comprehend or duplicate despite all our years of study. Humans are able to create wards that divert certain individuals away from a place or an object; they do this sometimes by illusion and sometimes by distraction. This is true of both Gray Book Marks and warlock magic. If a mundane passes through the Idris wards, however, he will be transported instantly to the corresponding location on the opposite border. This happens without any side effects or signs, so a mundane will have no awareness that he has passed instantly through an entire country. From the perspective of mundanes, it is as if Europe exists with no Idris in it at all, and indeed, this is how mundane maps depict things.

The wards of Idris were created by Raziel himself, as part of the initial set of gifts that he presented to Jonathan Shadowhunter. Their magic was not, apparently, magic that Raziel decided to share with his creations the Nephilim, and so we are unable to duplicate elsewhere, or at all modify, the wards of the Idris borders. Over the years Nephilim have argued endlessly about why the Idris wards allow the free passage of Downworlders and even demons themselves into Idris. In other words the wards prevent the discovery of Idris by the mundane world, but all members of the Shadow World may pass in and out freely. Many Shadowhunters have argued that Raziel's purpose in warding Idris was to prevent the Nephilim from ever becoming involved in land conflicts with its neighbors. Idris is meant as a hidden sanctuary from the mundane, and as a home, not as a political entity among the nations of the world, and as such, its borders can never be altered.

IDRIS AND THE MODERN WORLD

Idris's unspoiled nature is maintained in part by its wards, but strict Law also prevents the country from becoming modernized. This is partly because such improvements would be unworkable: magic easily disrupts modern technology. The wards that prevent mundanes from being able to enter or even detect Idris cause the whole country to exist in a "magical cage" that prevents machinery from working reliably within its borders. (This is similar to the disruption that prevents Marked firearms from functioning, and indeed, no firearm can be successfully fired within Idris.) As such,

Alicante is lit and powered primarily by witchlight, as are those rare roads that have been illuminated.

IDRIS AND DOWNWORLDERS

Idris is home to a number of Downworlder groups—faerie courts, werewolf packs in the forests, vampire clans in caves or in dark rocky valleys. For these Downworlders, Idris provides a space where they can live freely without having to disguise their identities, and where they can have land of their own, under their control. Those who live in Idris tend to be among the wildest of Downworlders, since they are the ones most willing to renounce the human world and live entirely away from mundanes. (This is even true for faeries, who, despite their prickliness, have a real affinity for humans and usually prefer to live among them.)

On the rare occasion when it has been necessary to bring an individual mundane into Idris for a moment of collaboration, or as part of Ascension proceedings, a Portal has proved the only method of circumventing the wards.

LAKE LYN

Other than Alicante the most sacred site for Shadowhunters in Idris is Lake Lyn, sometimes called the Lake of Dreams. It is the location where the Angel Raziel first appeared to Jonathan Shadowhunter, rising out of the waters and bearing the Cup, Sword, and Mirror that birthed our warrior race. Though the lake is sacred, its waters are in some way cursed: While Downworlders can drink from it safely, Shadowhunters who do so will suffer fevers, hallucinations, and sometimes, in severe cases, permanent madness. A Shadowhunter who has drunk from Lake Lyn can be healed with the use of healing Marks and other interventions, but they must be treated quickly, before the water has been absorbed fully into the system and cannot be drawn out again.

The shores of Lake Lyn give way to Brocelind Plain, a flat terrain of high grasses, which leads, as one heads toward Alicante, to Brocelind Forest. Writings tell us that the forest used to be much larger and covered the majority of the lowlands of Idris. Much of it was cleared as Alicante grew from being a small settlement in the center of a ring of demon towers to a large, bustling city. More of the forest was cleared to keep an easily patrolled border of open land around the city; Brocelind Forest has for hundreds of years been a favorite hiding place for vampire nests and werewolf packs. *ITS THE MIRROR. EVERYONE. Seriously, how did it take hundreds of years to figure this out?*

Never came up.

──── ALICANTE ────

Alicante, the Glass City. The holy city of the Nephilim. For Shadowhunters, Alicante is Jerusalem and Rome and Mecca and Shamballa and Bodh Gaya all in one. This must never be forgotten: While daily life goes on in the city as in any other, full of routine human needs and exchanges, it is the Forbidden City, the place given only to Nephilim as our base of operations and our haven on Earth.

To that end its towers protect it from demons, who cannot pass through the wards. Downworlders are able to pass through the wards without difficulty (a common argument for many years in favor of Downworlders' status as humans with souls, rather than demons), but they may not enter Alicante without permission. They are allowed to enter only as an invited guest of a Shadowhunter, and must either be accompanied by the Shadowhunter or carry with them the appropriate enchanted signed paperwork. (It is possible that you yourself have been through this process, if you were lucky enough to visit Alicante prior to your Ascension.) By tradition Downworlders are permitted to enter the city only through its north gate, which is guarded night and day.

In addition, for security reasons new Portals may not be opened directly into Alicante. Despite the partially demonic origin of the Portal, Shadowhunters have grown used to its convenience, and so typically Portals are opened to the outskirts of Alicante, outside the walls. The only exception is the permanent Portal in the Gard (see page 208). Shadowhunters often grumble about it, but the prohibition remains: Portals are created by warlocks, and while we are allied with warlocks as a group, we could not leave a hole in our defenses that would allow any possible rogue to open a Portal directly into our sanctum sanctorum.

FEATURES OF ALICANTE

The city is found in a shallow valley and divided by its river. The construction is mostly in gold- and honey-colored stone, with red tile roofs. Alicante rises up the side of a steep hill on one side, and its houses pile atop one another. From the river, canals have been dug, of which the largest is Princewater Canal. The new Shadowhunter is encouraged to stroll down Princewater Street and stand upon Oldcastle Bridge, from which the sound of the lapping water of the canal will accompany your excellent view of both the Gard and the Great Hall.

Apart from its unusual demon towers, Alicante is a city of canals. Since wells must be kept shallow to avoid piercing the *adamas* veins below the city, and the *adamas* provides a similar problem for Roman-style aqueducts, for many hundreds of years most fresh water was brought into the city by a series of artificial canals, crossed by Alicante's distinctive arched stone bridges. Today a network of underground pipes allows for running water in most Alicante homes, and its canals remain as reminders of an older age and as a charming feature of the city.

THE DEMON TOWERS

The demon towers of Alicante are Idris's most dramatic physical feature, a true wonder of the world. With the towers soaring into the sky like the finials of a heavenly crown, formed of pure *adamas*, it seems impossible that they could have been made by human hands. And in fact our history teaches us that they were not: The accounts of Jonathan Shadowhunter that have come down to us suggest that they were brought into being by Raziel, and that they grow out of a thick vein of *adamas* placed by Raziel under the earth to be mined for our Nephilim weapons and tools.

Raziel's words to Jonathan Shadowhunter include, in addition to the discussion of the Mortal Instruments, a mention of "a gift I bring to you upon the Earth." It's been often thought that this refers to the carving (and warding) of Idris out of the wilderness in the southern part of the Holy Roman Empire, but others have argued that it refers to the demon towers.

All Shadowhunters should look to the demon towers to remind themselves of their appointed station. These warded spires are a constant reminder that we are chosen and protected by the Angel, and that we are not entirely alone in our mission.

The demon towers have stood unchanged since the time of the very first Shadowhunters. Unlike with all other examples of worked *adamas*, their glow does not diminish with use, and their power has no need of being refreshed. Scholars have worked to determine why this might be, and whether the towers behave like normal *adamas* in other ways—whether they could be disabled by a dark ritual, whether they could be Marked, and so on. The towers remain the greatest lasting mystery of Raziel, and one that those in Alicante will find themselves contemplating as they pass under the towers' shadows. *Next Codex revision—demon towers less majestic and mysterious. More reminder of bad stuff.*

THE GARD

Yeah, this part seems a little naive now.

The Gard is the official meeting place of the Clave. It is the home of the Consul and Inquisitor and their families, and it is where the Law is made and debated. When the Clave is officially in session, only adult Shadowhunters are allowed onto its grounds.

The building is of dark stone and is basic in its architecture—a simple fortress, built for safety and supported on all sides by undecorated pillars. (Undecorated by architectural features, that is; the pillars are of course extensively inscribed with protective Marks.) Four demon towers, smaller than the ones that guard the city, rise from the four cardinal points of the building. Legend tells us that it was to the center of these demon towers that Raziel brought Jonathan Shadowhunter before telling him, "This is where your work shall begin." The Gard is thus believed to be on the site of the original small settlement that became Alicante, although the original structures are long gone; earlier generations did not have the reverence for history that we do now.

The gates of the Gard are among its most dramatic features; several times taller than a man, they are wrought from a combination of silver and cold iron, and are covered in calligraphic

208

interpretations of Marks. On either side of the gates stand the stone statues, known colloquially as the Guardians. Each is a warrior-angel holding a carved sword and standing above a dying creature meant to represent the demonic enemies of the Nephilim—a reminder that angels are beautiful, but also terrible, and that just as we are in part angel, so are we warriors.

There is only one Portal open in Alicante, and it is in the Gard, for the use of the Clave in times of emergency. The potential danger of this "back door" is mitigated by this Portal's being "reverse-warded" in the manner of an Institute's Sanctuary. That is, Marks block it off as a place outside the protection of wards. The demonic magic involved in Portal construction can function inside this one room of the Gard, much as a vampire could stand safely in the Sanctuary of an Institute. This of course represents a large potential security risk, and so the exact location of the Portal is a closely guarded secret.

ANGEL SQUARE AND THE GREAT HALL

One of Alicante's most picturesque and historically relevant spots is the plaza located at the city's center, Angel Square, known for the bronze statue of the Angel Raziel that stands at the heart of the square. It is the largest statue of Raziel in the world, although one can find many smaller copies of it in Institutes around the globe. (Many of these claim to be recasts of the original sculpture, and some are, but others are definitely not; this distinction is, however, of interest only to historians of Shadowhunter art and thus will not be addressed in detail here.)

At the northern end of the square stands the Great Hall of the Angel, built in the eighteenth century as a general meeting hall for all Shadowhunters. This neoclassical edifice, with its long marble staircase and its magnificent pillared arcade, is a symbol of the enduring strength and integrity of the Nephilim.

In 1872 the Great Hall was used as the location for the historic signing of the First Accords, since Downworlders are not being permitted to enter the Gard. This signing marked the first occasion when Downworlders were permitted into Alicante in large groups; they entered the city through the north gate as is traditional. Since the signing, the building has been commonly referred to as the Accords Hall, and it continues to be used every fifteen years for the revising and signing of the Accords. In other times it is the site of celebrations, ceremonies, weddings, and festivals.

The majority of the interior of the Hall is taken up by a single large room, the site of these ceremonies; its walls are pale white and its ceiling high, with a large glass skylight that allows natural sunlight in. In the center of the room stands a large fountain in the shape of a mermaid, commissioned and sculpted in 1902 to celebrate the Third Accords, the first of the new century.

THE ARMORY

The Armory is an imposing stone stronghold on the eastern side of Alicante, part storehouse, part museum, part research center. It represents the only presence of the Iron Sisters within Idris proper, although visitors rarely see them, since the Sisters spend most of their time below ground level, working on new weapon designs, performing repairs, and the like. The Armory serves the same function for Alicante as the weapons room does for an Institute. The Clave has the authority to take whatever weaponry they need from it to outfit Shadowhunters for conflict within Idris. Those who are not Clave members are restricted to the south wing, which serves as a museum of antiquated weapons no longer in use, and showcases a small collection of weapons made famous in Shadowhunter legend.

The building was constructed in a medieval style, echoing fortress imagery, with its high stone walls lined in turrets. However, it dates only from the early 1800s and was built in a self-consciously antiquated style. The interior is not at all laid out like a fortress, and the impression that it gives of being able to withstand artillery fire is mostly a surface affectation. The Iron Sisters are protected instead by doing their work in its extensive and labyrinthine basement levels. A passage somewhere in those basement levels is said to lead directly to the Adamant Citadel.

THE SILENT CITY

For many Shadowhunters the Silent City is something taken for granted, a home for the Silent Brothers and a complex city of levels and chambers that has always been there, that has been inhabited for eternity. In truth the Silent City constitutes one of the great engineering feats of its millennium, on par with the building of the greatest of mundane cathedrals and temples.

THE BUILDING OF THE SILENT CITY

The actual construction of the Silent City was undertaken by the Silent Brothers, and it took roughly four hundred years for the City to attain its current size and reach. It began as a cavern of worked stone in the mysterious non-geographical space beneath Idris, no more than a small council chamber, a small area used as living quarters, and the earliest Shadowhunter graveyard. That is how David the Silent described it. At that point, of course, it would not have been described as a city. It became known to Shadowhunters as the Silent Cloister and was slowly expanded over the first hundred years or so of the Shadowhunters. Although it had become much larger than its original state, it was still more like a great underground manor house than like a city. Residences for the earliest Silent Brothers had been moved to a separate level; the area for gravesites had been, inevitably, expanded; and the Sword-Chamber, as it was then known, was larger and more imposing.

THE CITY EXPANDS

In roughly 1300 the first two entrances to the Silent Cloister were built outside Idris: one in what is now the city of Bangalore, in southern India, and one in the city of Heidelberg, in what is now southern Germany. Both were created to allow Silent Brothers much easier access to the extensive research materials those cities contained; the Silent Brothers also began to recruit for their ranks among the mundane monks and scholars who either lived in or traveled to those cities for wisdom.

At this point construction and expansion of the Silent Cloisters accelerated rapidly. Already by 1402, Council records referred to "That Great City, whose levels we know not and whose secrets the Brothers keep in Silence." The means by which the Silent Brothers were excavating their city, and even the location on Earth where this extensive city resided, was a closely guarded secret. It remains one of the mysteries that only Silent Brothers are permitted to know. (It's widely believed that the Iron Sisters assisted in the construction presumably by building devices for digging and construction. The Iron Sisters, however, keep their secrets just as faultlessly as the Silent Brothers.) Specific historical details are few, but we do know that the prisons of the Nephilim were moved from an outbuilding of the Gard in Alicante (now long demolished) to the deepest levels of the City in 1471, and that the council chamber that most Shadowhunters who have visited the City have seen was completed and opened to Shadowhunters in 1536. Construction and expansion continued after that, however. In fact, we cannot say for sure that the Silent Brothers are not *still* expanding, building their City ever larger; we have no proof either way.

VISITING THE SILENT CITY

Most Shadowhunters only ever see the two upper levels of the City—its archives, and its council chamber, where the Soul-Sword resides. There are, however, levels upon levels, plunging deep into the earth. The vast majority of these levels are off-limits to anyone who is not a Silent Brother, and the details of the Silent Brothers' living quarters, sustenance, laboratories, etc., remain a closely guarded secret. The exceptions are at the lowest depths of the city, where a series of levels holds the necropolis of the Shadowhunters and thousands and thousands of our people are laid to rest. And below these, on the very lowest levels, are the prisons.

The prisons of the Silent City can hold the living, the undead, and the dead; they are designed to constrain all creatures, however magical. (The exceptions here are demons, who may be powerful enough to break out of even the strongest cells.) Where those guilty of lesser violations may be incarcerated in Alicante, or in the keeps of Institutes, the cells of the Silent City are reserved only for the worst of Lawbreakers and the most dangerous of wrongdoers. Pray that you never need see them yourself.

SILENT CITY: NOT A TRANSIT HUB!

Since there are entrances to the Silent City all over the globe, one might reasonably ask whether the city provides Shadowhunters with a convenient route for travel. One could presumably travel quickly between distant places by, say, entering the Silent City in New York City and exiting in Tokyo. Indeed, Silent Brothers do use the Silent City's entrances in this fashion, so that they can be rapidly deployed where they are needed. Iron Sisters, too, are permitted to use the City this way, although they are rarely seen outside their Citadel. Regular Shadowhunters are not permitted, by tradition and Law, to use the City as a glorified train station. The general consensus is that this would not be a good idea, as it would likely involve passing through parts of the Silent City that the Nephilim who are not Brothers would find too horrifying to experience without losing their minds. This may or may not be true, but the Silent Brothers have done nothing to deny the rumors.

— THE ADAMANT CITADEL —

As the Silent Brothers carefully keep the secrets of their City, most Shadowhunters know even less about the Adamant Citadel, the home of the Iron Sisters. In many ways it is simpler, of course, since it is a single fortress rather than an entire city. On the other hand its mysteries are such that, for all we know, it could extend as extensively and as deeply as the Silent City; its inner chambers may be walked by only the Sisters themselves.

The Adamant Citadel stands on a volcanic plain, a stretch of dried lava beds, black and forbidding; a narrow river of molten lava rings it like a moat. It is reached—like the Silent City—through one of a number of entrances scattered around the world, the oldest of which resides on the lowest floor of the Armory in Alicante. The volcanic activity serves as a convenient defense for the Citadel, of course, but the location was probably selected to provide the Sisters with the extreme heat that they require for their forges.

The Portals that lead to the Citadel will not take you directly into the fortress, but rather to the volcanic plain, outside the walls. A ring of smooth, unbroken *adamas*, many times taller than a person, surrounds the Citadel; this ring, which appears to be a single continuous band of *adamas*, with no signs of mortaring or structural engineering, is an imposing sight, a reminder that the Iron Sisters are not simple blacksmiths but rather are working with seraphic forces that we can barely comprehend. In the walls is set one gate, formed of two gigantic blades that cross each other to form a pointed arch. This gate is normally left open but can be closed and sealed in times of emergency.

Through the gate, however, the fortress is still well protected. The actual Citadel building can be reached only by crossing a drawbridge, which can be lowered only by a small sacrifice of blood from a female Shadowhunter. The bridge is strewn with knives, embedded blade-upward, which must be carefully avoided. It is therefore not possible to approach the Adamant Citadel in haste; its gates cannot be stormed and its walls cannot be laid siege to.

The fortress is a dramatic structure, soaring into the gray skies above the lava plain, with a ring of towers around it that call to mind the demon towers of Alicante, though these are more regular and less graceful, having been constructed by the hands of humans. The towers are tipped with glittering electrum, but otherwise the whole structure is of *adamas*, glowing gently with white-silver light.

Once in the fortress a visitor would find herself in the antechamber—and this is all of the Adamant Citadel that those other than Iron Sisters are permitted to see. The antechamber is a simple room; the walls glow with *adamas*, as does the floor and the ceiling far above. In the floor is a black circle in which is carved the sigil of the Iron Sisters: a heart pierced by a blade. There are no furnishings or comforts; the Iron Sisters do not appreciate visitors and will endeavor to complete their business as rapidly as possible.

The walls of the Adamant Citadel are like the lives of the Iron Sisters themselves: hard, unyielding, and strong. Their motto, and the motto of the Citadel, makes this clear: *ignis aurum probat.* "Fire tests gold."

The Iron Sisters seem pretty awesome.

If by "awesome" you mean "completely terrifying," then yes, agreed.

INSTITUTES OF THE CLAVE

At first, there was no need for Institutes. For a few dozen years after the birth of the Nephilim, all the Shadowhunters in the world could reach the gates of Alicante in, at most, two or three days' ride. But we were created to be a global organization, and it quickly became necessary for outposts to be built, places of angelic power where Shadowhunters could organize and remain safe. And so were created the Institutes, the local power bases of the Nephilim.

Institutes function like the embassies of mundane governments. They are Nephilim homes, as much as Idris itself is. Crossing the threshold into an Institute, you are no longer in the country or state or city that the Institute's building stands in, but are rather in Nephilim land, where our Law is predominant.

The corollary to this is that Institutes are the responsibility of all Shadowhunters, not just the Shadowhunters who are stationed at a particular Institute or who are a part of the Conclave of that Institute's region. The oaths we take to protect our lands extend to all Institutes, around the world.

There are some features common to all Institutes. They are built on hallowed ground and are heavily warded. They are constructed to repel demons and to prevent the unhallowed from entering. Their doors remain locked to anyone lacking Nephilim blood. (The reverse is also true: The doors are open to anyone possessing Nephilim blood.) The mortar for the buildings' stones are mixed with the blood of Shadowhunters, the wooden beams are of rowan, and the nails are of silver, iron, or electrum.

Never has the invention of the regional office been treated so melodramatically.

Mmm delicious blood | eat your Institute nom nom nom

Very mature, Lewis. 217

Aside from these commonalities, one can find Institutes of all shapes and sizes, from the single-story sprawling villa of the Mexico City *Instituto* to the Eastern Carpathian Mountains fortress *Institut* high above Cluj in Romania. Each continent has an Institute that contains the Great Library for that region of the world; each of these is the largest Institute on its respective continent. These are: London, in Europe; Shanghai, in Asia; Manila, in Oceania (which region encompasses Australia and the Pacific Rim); Cairo, in Africa; São Paulo, in South America; and Los Angeles, in North America. Each of these larger Institutes has the capacity to house hundreds of Shadowhunters, although most Shadowhunters do not permanently live in an Institute. Normally, even the largest of Institutes has only a small number of permanent residents, who are responsible for maintaining the premises and equipment.

All local Shadowhunters will be called to their Institute for Enclave meetings, to discuss local affairs that need not involve the Clave or Council. In some parts of the world, the head of the local Enclave is always the head of the largest local Institute; in some places they are different persons. Local traditions and history dominate; the only requirement is that the region be adequately represented in the Clave, however the local organization is structured.

THE CONSTRUCTION OF INSTITUTES

Shadowhunter Institutes are built to serve as symbols of the power and sanctity of the Nephilim; they should stand as monuments to the Angel and glorifications of our mission. Often they include architectural elements meant to evoke well-known buildings in Alicante. There are many smaller copies of the Gard's Council Hall wooden doors, for instance.

Typically, and especially in well-populated areas, Institutes are glamoured to blend in with their surroundings. This glamour is usually chosen to make the Institute look not only ordinary but unappealing to visitors. For instance, the Institute of New York City, though in truth a magnificent Gothic-style cathedral, is glamoured to appear as a broken-down, boarded-up church, a derelict awaiting demolition.

Although the wards of the demon towers of Alicante prevent electricity and similar power sources from working reliably inside its borders, the weaker wards of Institutes typically do not cause this problem. Most Institutes today are wired for electricity, or at worst gaslight, although witchlight is often used for atmospheric effect or as a backup in places where electrical supply may be unreliable. There are exceptions, of course—a few of the Institutes in more historically besieged areas, or more remote locations, are either too warded or too far from mundane civilization to use modern power sources.

Institutes do not have keyed locks, except out of historical preservation. Instead any Shadowhunter may gain entrance to any Institute by putting her hand to the door and requesting entrance in the name of the Clave and the Angel Raziel.

SANCTUARIES

Most Institutes built before the 1960s contain Sanctuaries. Sanctuaries are meant to solve an obvious problem with the Nephilim practice of building Institutes on sanctified ground. While doing so prevents demons from entering an Institute, it also prevents all Downworlders from entering. There was a time when this policy was a wise one, but it creates the problem of preventing Institutes from holding a Downworlder temporarily—for example when there's a need to interrogate one, and incarceration in the Silent City would be more complicated than the situation warranted. Then too, in this modern age the Nephilim maintain cordial relations with many Downworlders, who assist us with information. To solve this problem Sanctuaries— unsanctified spaces that connect directly to the sanctified spaces of Institutes—were attached to most Institutes. Here Downworlders may be held or, as the case may be, hosted. Sanctuaries are typically well-protected and warded, typically by mundane key and by Mark as well.

Projection magic was invented by an unnamed warlock (or team of warlocks, possibly) on the Indian subcontinent in 1958, and spread quickly through the world, mostly obviating the need for Sanctuaries. Most Institutes, however, predate that year, and their Sanctuaries have been maintained as contingencies and out of historical interest.

NYC Institute has one. I'll show you sometime if you want.

It's a date.

It is maybe the least romantic spot in the Institute, by the way.

You'll make up for that, I'm sure.

JEEZ, GET A LOCKED ROOM ON UNSANCTIFIED GROUND, YOU TWO.

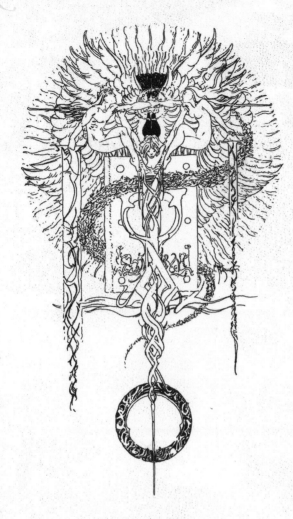

EXCERPTS FROM
A HISTORY OF
THE NEPHILIM

— BEFORE THE NEPHILIM —

We cannot say much about the origin of demons. All we can say for sure is that they were in our world well before humans came to be.

In the beginning was the world, and light, and humanity, and goodness, but in the beginning too were the demons, Sammael and Lilith, mother and father of evil to come, the paragons of corruption and sin. They were created when the world was created, and roamed freely, creating other, lesser demons, sowing chaos. They mated with humans and created warlocks. Their kind mated with angels, who in those times could be found on Earth, and created faeries. Sammael took the form of a great Serpent and tempted humanity into iniquity. Lilith, first wife of Adam, rejected the ways of mortals and cursed their children to torment. Or so say the oldest texts of the Nephilim. THE NEWER ONES SAY THEY WERE A SONG-AND-DANCE TEAM. We get it, you don't have a clue.

The history of demons is murky and mythological in nature. Within the Jewish, Christian, and Muslim traditions there are dozens of variations on the story of these two ur-demons and their offspring, and in other major religious traditions there are tales that may or may not be discussing the same entities. All religions, after all, have a tradition of demonology. We can say only that at some time around the very beginnings of humanity, the demons grew too strong and too many, and Heaven declared war on them. Heaven won the war, but the angels were unable to eradicate demons from the world. They had to be satisfied with banishing demonkind to the Void, and they modified our world in some subtle way unknown to us, which made it dangerously toxic to demons, preventing their return.

Nephilimic folklore tells us that this war between Heaven and the demons decimated Earth, and that the mythological objects of human religion—the Tower of Babel, the Garden of Eden, the World-Tree, the original pyramids—were wiped away by the destruction. So too were the supernatural animals of mythology, the unicorn and the dragon among them. We cannot know, of course, the truth of it. All we can say for sure is that the faeries survived.

Time passed. Stability came to Earth, and human history as we know it began. Demons were mostly kept out of our world, since they could not survive its poisonous effect on their bodies for long. Some of the more powerful demons could remain for a matter of hours or even days. Eventually, however, they would fall apart as their energies were snapped back to the Void. Humanity cursed what evil it found, not knowing the peace they luxuriated in.

WARLOCKS AND FEY: THE EARLIEST DOWNWORLDERS

The fey are the oldest race of Downworlders in existence; they are known, in fact, to precede humans by eons, although it is assumed that they were very different in those early days. Warlocks are almost as old a group. They were very few in number, but some individual demons were able to survive in our world long enough to create warlocks. Only through these warlocks did humans know anything of demonic magic.

WARLOCKS BEFORE THE NEPHILIM

It was a warlock who was the first Downworlder that Jonathan Shadowhunter directly interacted with—Elphas the Unsteady. Elphas wrote the earliest known "Nephilim-approved" demonology, compiling data from his and the

first-generation Shadowhunters' personal experiences
and offering extensive commentary on other earlier
demonologies, since new Shadowhunters often would
possess some "foreknowledge of Downworld" that
turned out to be entirely false and based on popular,
incorrect texts.

There are today eight warlocks living
who claim to have been born earlier than
Jonathan Shadowhunter. Of these, scholars
believe that five are probably credible, and
of those, two have enough corroborating
evidence to indicate that they're telling
the truth. One of these, Baba Agnieszka,
is known to be the elder sister of Elphas
the Unsteady and has lived quietly in
Idris since 1452, in a cottage built and
maintained for her by the Nephilim in
honor of her family connection. She is
unfriendly to visitors and appears to prefer
to be left alone. Recent reports from those
who have visited her have described her as
mad and doddering, which is not normally
something that happens to warlocks.

Agnieszka appears to have deteriorated mentally not as
a result of physical aging but rather due to a slow decay
caused by eccentricity and isolation. She is something of a
relic, but to the Nephilim she is a holy relic.

The other verified ancient living warlock is far older
than Agnieszka. Isaac Laquedem's birth has been traced to
what is now southwestern France, in the early part of the
seventh century. He became known widely for his warlock
mark, a large and impressive set of stag's antlers. The

legends of a man with antlers who rode on a hunt across France, never resting in one place, are likely to originate with him. Early French Shadowhunters, who were sure that the Wandering Hunter was a myth or at best a composite of a number of different figures, were astonished to meet Laquedem and discover not only that he was real but that the stories about him were almost entirely true.

Laquedem's hunting days have come to an end, and he chooses to live out his eternity on a farm not far from Bergerac in France. Despite his age Laquedem is useless as a source of historical knowledge on any topic except the forests of France, about which he knows an enormous amount. The rest of history has largely passed Laquedem by.

WE MUST GO HANG OUT WITH THAT GUY! He's actually pretty boring. Also hope you like
No! eating a lot of venison.

THE INCURSION
Always have to one-up me, don't y
You magnificent bastard.

The demon Incursion, their large-scale invasion of our world, began shortly after the first Christian Millennium (that is, AD 1000) and has not yet ceased.

After what seemed like thousands of years of dormancy, Lilith and Sammael awoke and—so the story goes—performed a demonic ritual, of enormous power, that could be performed only once and never again. The ritual affected the whole of the

demon city Pandemonium, and with this act they massively strengthened all of demonkind's resistance to the toxicity of our world. After the ritual, demons were still poisoned by our world, but to a much lesser degree, and demons began to enter our world and remain here for long periods of time, drinking the life from it and bringing with them ruination and rot. They invaded, and humanity suffered.

CRUSADES AND CULTS

The Incursion was disastrous for humanity, in more ways than one. The most obvious consequence was the sheer physical damage, of course—demons wiped out whole villages, burned crops, turned brothers against one another.

But the more extensive damage lay in humanity's response to the threat. The presence of demons gave rise to apocalyptic cults that disrupted the normal structures of life and religion. Some cults were demon-worshippers, hoping to be spared by their conquerors. Other cults tried to band together to fight the demons, usually bringing destruction upon themselves and anyone unlucky enough to be close by. These cults spread fear and chaos where they went.

Worse, perhaps, than isolated apocalyptic cults was the larger political response. Christian Europe decided that the demons were spreading over their lands because their Holy Land of Jerusalem was not in Christian hands, and declared the first Crusades in order to get it back. Thus, rather than turning their attention to the immediate demonic threat, the Islamic Near East and the Christian West entered a long series of bloody wars and recriminations that, if anything, only helped the demons spread mayhem and death.

JONATHAN SHADOWHUNTER

The Crusades soon became a popular career path for young men of Europe seeking their fortune and name in battle. It was an opportunity for renown. Some, like Jonathan Shadowhunter, were younger sons of nobles and would not inherit their family's fortune. Jonathan felt pulled to battle because of honor and duty, surely, but the Crusades also were one of the few avenues available to him.

Unfortunately, the man Jonathan is something of an enigma to us today. We know little of his life before the Nephilim and even less of his childhood or family of origin. (A medieval tradition tells us that he was the seventh son of a seventh son, but no evidence of this exists.) We know that his family were wealthy landowners but he would inherit nothing from them.

Of the fateful trip that changed his life and our whole world, we know that Jonathan was on his way to Constantinople to join the European forces mustering there. He traveled not alone but with two companions: David, his closest friend, who hoped to join the Crusade not as a soldier but as a medic; and Abigail, Jonathan's elder sister, bound too for Constantinople, not to fight but to join the man to whom she was betrothed. (Of this doomed fiancé no knowledge remains, except that Jonathan was unhappy with the match and often spoke about his pleasure at Abigail remaining with him rather than wasting away "in some tiny hamlet on the Black Sea.")

A NOTE ON JONATHAN SHADOWHUNTER'S ORIGINS

While the story of the creation of the Nephilim is one that has been told and retold continually since that creation, there are several key details of Jonathan Shadowhunter himself that are, frustratingly, lost to history. His home prior to his encounter with Raziel is known only to be somewhere in central, northern, or western Europe, because at the time his journey was interrupted. David reports that their party was traveling east. Over the course of history almost every nation has made a claim as the home of Jonathan Shadowhunter; there was a powerful faction in the eighteenth century that believed him to have been a massive Icelandic warrior, for instance, though we now believe that theory is somewhat far-fetched.

A DREAM OF SHADOWS

Our only direct report from the group that beheld Raziel comes from translations of accounts supposedly written by David. It's not known whether he wrote these accounts as they were happening or wrote them as memoirs later in his life. They are, however, the closest we can come to the truth.

In his notes David relates a conversation that, he says, took place the night before the creation of the Nephilim. The three travelers were camped in the forest. Several days before, they had met and fought a small lone demon on the road. They did manage to chase it off, but not without Jonathan suffering a deep, dangerous wound in his right arm. The wound was thickly bandaged, and Jonathan held his arm immobilized in a sling, but then, by the light of a small, almost smokeless fire, he unwrapped the bandages from his arm, and he said to his companions, "This cut is deep and long. The demons have put such a wound into the flesh of the world itself, which can be bandaged, but under the bandages it will not heal."

Abigail agreed that this was true, but that the three of them, young and inexperienced, had little power to help. David remained silent, as was his preference, staring into the fire and considering.

Jonathan continued, "It does not work simply to kill demons. They damage the world by their very presence. They must be eliminated, the wound of the world bound and dressed so that it might begin to heal."

He told them of a dream: "On the night that I pledged my sword to the Crusades," he said, "I dreamed I stood in blazing sunlight, golden like the light of heaven, and my sword shone so that I myself was blinded. On the night my arm suffered this scratch, I dreamed differently. I had realized that the demons I sought would not come to me, in the light. They remained safe in darkness, and their power lay in keeping their secrets.

"In this dream I still held my sword, but it did not shine. Instead I crept through the shadows, which embraced me like a child. The shadows became not the demons' ally but mine. When I

233

struck with my sword, it was with silence and speed, and none but myself and the demon knew what had transpired."

We cannot know whether the events that led to the creation of the Nephilim were destined, or were manipulated into place by Heaven, or just arose by chance. Whether the world would have been destroyed without Jonathan Shadowhunter, or whether some other leader would have arisen, is a matter for speculation. The fact is that in the hour of greatest need, Jonathan Shadowhunter did rise up and become that leader.

LAKE LYN

The next day (according to David), the party's travels took them to Lake Lyn, in the mountains of Central Europe. The lake was not the glittering blue of today but a black roiling tear in the fabric of the world through which demons passed back and forth freely. Jonathan, David, and Abigail were attacked there by a swarm of demons, of some species we can't now identify. (There are a few possibilities supported by different scholars, but all we have is David's description—"very large, like a bat and a shadow, an eagle and a serpent, that towered over us like a thunderstorm." *Idiots. Obviously it was a swarm of serpent-eagle Thundershadowbats.*

The party fought the demons back as best they could, but Jonathan was already wounded, and neither Abigail nor David possessed great physical strength. David tells us that Jonathan threw off his sling and bandages and fought valiantly through the pain. They held the demons off from killing them, but were overwhelmed. Finally the demons took all three into the lake, to drown them.

Fighting against his fate, Jonathan used what little breath he had to ask a blessing on the lake, to sanctify it as a place where things of evil, such as these demons, would not be welcome. He prayed, and his prayer was answered.

234

Suuuuuuure

RAZIEL AND THE MORTAL INSTRUMENTS

And Raziel rose from the lake, bearing with him the Mortal Instruments. All action ceased. Even the demonic energies of the tear in the world seemed to stop. In the forests surrounding them, birds quit their singing.

Raziel spoke, saying, *Be not afraid.*

I am an angel of the Lord come unto you, Jonathan. You have called me and I have come.

Jonathan said, "Please, save my friends."

We cannot blame Jonathan for not asking Raziel for a greater gift; indeed it is admirable that in such a moment he would think first of the lives of his companions.

Raziel lifted Jonathan, David, and Abigail from the lake and placed them on the shore. The Angel's figure was human, but so

235

large that he could cradle the three mortals easily in his palms.

Then he lifted his arms, and with a single great motion he flung the remaining demons high into the air. Jonathan watched them rise and rise, eventually fading to pinpricks that vanished against the stars. Then Raziel turned his gaze back to Jonathan. *I know your dream,* he said. Rᴀᴢɪᴇʟ ᴛʜʀᴇᴡ ᴛʜᴇᴍ INTO SPACE. Aᴡᴇsᴏᴍᴇ.

Jonathan was struck silent. He looked to his friends, and saw that they were not conscious but were breathing.

On the banks of the lake, Raziel placed the Cup, the Sword, and the Mirror, and told Jonathan each of their functions. Beside them he placed his Book, and he told Jonathan the function of this as well. With his finger he gently inscribed across the wound in Jonathan's arm the first *iratze* seen on Earth. Jonathan watched in awe as his flesh again became unbroken, as if the natural order of the world briefly moved backward, and the pain of the injury subsided. He bowed his head and gave thanks. Then Raziel lifted the Cup and in it he mixed his angelic blood and the blood of Jonathan, and he said: *In your dream you saw a great truth—that to destroy the things of darkness, it is sometimes necessary to descend into the shadows to join them. You shall bring men and women into the darkness with you, and you will master the shadows, and you will hunt.*

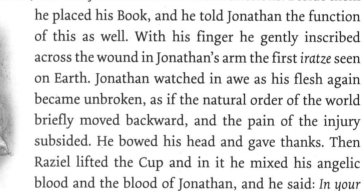

From now until the end of the world,
You shall be called Jonathan Shadowhunter
For you and your kin will drive the shadows of the world away
And you will make light in dark places
And you will be called Nephilim, as it says in the book of Genesis:

"The Nephilim were in the earth in those days, and also after that, when the sons of God came unto the daughters of men, and they bore children to them: the same were the mighty men that were of old, the men of renown."

For you will be of men and yet you will be of angels; both in one.

Raziel seemed less annoyed with everybody back then.

Dealing with humans for the last thousand years probably hasn't helped his mood.

IDRIS

The Angel Raziel, in his generosity, had two more gifts for Jonathan Shadowhunter.

The first was the gift of *adamas*, the heavenly crystal that glowed with heavenly fire, that could not be cut or carved by mundane means, and the secrets of whose working could be found only in the Gray Book. *Demons will recoil from its power,* said Raziel. *It shall be the metal of the Nephilim forevermore, however much is needed.* And he presented to Jonathan a polished branch of *adamas*, the first stele. *With this will you draw the sigils of Heaven.*

Then he raised his hands, and from the ground came spires and towers, many times the height of a man, spiked and yearning toward the sky. From many places on the plain they came, and when they had all grown, Raziel led these first Nephilim to a spot in the midst of the towers, where four smaller towers stood describing a diamond, and there he gave them the second gift, the gift of Idris.

This shall be your country, he said. *A haven for all the Nephilim and those who beat against the shadows of this world.* He described the wards he had created, and the safety they promised. And then he began to rise back toward Heaven. *Now never contact me again, he said.*

Legend tells us that then Jonathan Shadowhunter cried out in a moment of human weakness, asking Raziel how he could be called if the need became too great for mortals to bear. And Raziel answered him that he had given all he could, the many gifts of Heaven: the Cup, the Sword, the Mirror, the Gray Book, the *adamas*, the land of Idris. He could give no more. This mission, he said, must be the mission of men. But then he relented, and his sternness briefly faded, and he said, *If you again find yourself in true need—true need—of me, take the Cup, the Sword, the Mirror—these Mortal Instruments—and summon me by the shores of the lake.*

And then he departed. *But seriously, never call me.*

—— THE RISE OF THE NEPHILIM —— IN THE WORLD

We owe a great debt to the earliest Nephilim, Jonathan, David, and Abigail (for Jonathan's first task once Raziel had left was to nurse his friend and his sister back to health, and to have them drink water from the Mortal Cup to transform them, too, into Nephilim like himself). On their own, recruiting as they could from among locals and trusted associates, they laid the stones upon which all of Shadowhunter society was built.

Abigail Shadowhunter set the precedent for Shadowhunters comprising both men and women, a guiding principle that has continued to this day. With the intensity of a new Boadicea, she established that the female Shadowhunters were no less fierce and resolute than the men organized under Jonathan's banner. When she grew older, and could no longer wage war against demonkind as she once had, she turned to the esoteric knowledge of the Gray

Book and the beating angelic heart of *adamas* beneath Idris to become the first Iron Sister. Along with six other Nephilim she constructed the first *adamas* forge, and the earliest incarnation of the Adamant Citadel upon its volcanic plain.

David, by contrast, was never a warrior and always a scholar and medic. Early in his time among the Nephilim, he witnessed a ritual sacrifice performed by a Greater Demon in an anonymous cave in Idris, and the horror of what he saw caused him to take a permanent vow of silence. This sent him, too, to the farthest depths of the Gray Book, into deep research. Over time he and his followers grew away from the world, remaining Nephilim but sacrificing some of their humanity for more angelic power. David became the founder of the Silent Brothers, and with the help of the Iron Sisters, he exorcised the cave of his nightmares and created the beginnings of the Silent City.

Meanwhile, Jonathan and his followers went out into the world to recruit more worthy men and women to become Shadowhunters. When possible they recruited whole families, bringing them wholesale into the Nephilim and granting them new names, in the compound model of the Shadowhunters. There is, of course, scarce space in these pages to tell the stories of those early Shadowhunters, blazing their warrior's trails across Earth, but we encourage the interested Shadowhunter to seek out some of the more interesting tales in the library of their local Institute:

- The tale of the first Institute on the British Isles, in Cornwall, where the first Nephilim arriving with the Cup were believed to be wielding the Holy Grail, and whose

239

tales of bravery and vigor have become mixed up with the mundane folklore of the isles.

· The earliest European Nephilim to arrive in the New World, and their struggles to survive the harsh winters and totally unfamiliar demons. Many were slaughtered, and if not for the assistance of the first peoples of that continent and a small number of helpful warlocks among them, they would surely have perished.

· The massacres of the 1450s, when the Institute at Cluj in Transylvania changed from a small mountain backwater to the busiest and most treacherous Nephilim posting in the world.

· Patrick of Cumbria, who united faeries, Shadowhunters, and mundane earls across Ireland in 1199 to drive the demons out (and whose work was unfortunately undone by Henry VIII, who ended several hundred years of demonlessness in Ireland when he began to reassert English control over the kingdom of Ireland beginning in the 1530s).

· The great Scorpion-Riders of the Australian backcountry, in the mid-1600s.

· The doomed Dazzling Charge of 1732, when a crack squad of Nephilim warriors in central France discovered, to their horror, the ineffectiveness of firearms in fighting demons.

· The lost Ethiopian Nephilim, separated from the entire Clave and Idris for hundreds of years beginning in the 1300s, but who kept up the ways of the Shadowhunters, the knowledge of Marks, and the use of the seraph blades independently, until they rejoined the world body in the 1850s.

Oh, come on, these sound great. Codex gives fifty pages of demon history but not this interesting stuff?

240

So go find stuff in the library! That's what it's for.

CLARY, I HEREBY ORDER YOU TO GO READ ABOUT SCORPION-RIDERS, WHATEVER THEY ARE. SCORPION-RIDERS! THEY RIDE SCORPIONS! I ASSUME!

MUNDANE RELIGION AND THE NEPHILIM

In the earliest days of the Nephilim, their greatest worry was the possible negative response by the dominant religious-political powers in Europe at the time, the Catholic and the Eastern Orthodox churches. Both churches were very watchful through the Middle Ages for what they would consider heretical positions, and while many of their interests were aligned with the Nephilim's, we could not be said to in any way be in line with church orthodoxy. While local skirmishes sometimes broke out, the leadership of the churches and the Clave prevented any all-out battle.

It was, in fact, a difficult moment in history to recruit for a secret confraternity. There was a tremendous amount of competition, in the form of the various orders of religious knights that were appearing then in the world in the wake of the Crusades. The Knights Hospitaller were founded around the same time as the Nephilim; the Knights Templar in 1130; even the famed Assassins came about only in the 1090s. The Nephilim had to be very selective and chose to recruit only superlative candidates, "allowing" those they rejected to take vows in a military order. On the other hand, disappearing into the ranks of the Nephilim was not as difficult as it would be today, since such life-changing vows were fairly common.

In the course of the first several hundred years of the Nephilim, contacts were made between us and the more mystical orders of the world's major religions. A very small but well-chosen collection of religious leaders signed secret treaties to provide havens and weapons for Shadowhunters in exchange for protection.

I bet the church excommunicated the heck out of Jonathan, though.

Nope, they'd have had to make a public statement, officially they'd never heard of JS.

241

Warning: If you don't already know about this, it is some bad stuff.

— THE HUNTS AND THE SCHISM —

Many are the stories of noble Nephilim, stouthearted and powerful men and women who can inspire us today with the tales of their courage and valor. History is, however, not a storybook, and we would fail in our duty of instructing the new Shadowhunter if we ignored the more shameful and contemptible actions of our forebears. The Nephilim have always acted with morally upright objectives and out of a desire to do good in the world, but with our modern sensibilities we must mention, and condemn, those occasions when from those ambitions came behaviors that we would now consider to be evil.

The sixteenth and seventeenth centuries saw a tragic fad sweep through Europe: witch-hunting. It arose for a number of historical reasons—among them, religious fervor coinciding with the Protestant Reformation and a renewed interest on the part of the Catholic Church in condemning "devil-worship." What began as the lynching of innocent and mostly mundane women (and some men) as "witches" expanded quickly, to become official mundane law. England, for instance, passed the first version of its Witchcraft Act in 1542, which made it illegal to:

> . . . use devise practise or exercise, or cause to be used devysed practised or exercised, any Invocacons or conjuracons of Sprites wichecraftes enchauntmentes or sorceries, to thentent to get or fynde money or treasure, or to waste consume or destroy any persone in his bodie membres or goodes, or to pvoke [provoke]

243

any persone to unlawfull love, or for any other unlawfull intente or purpose . . . or for dispite of Cryste, or for lucre of money, dygge up or pull downe any Crosse or Crosses, or by suche Invocacons or conjuracons of Sprites wichecraftes enchauntementes or sorcerie or any of them take upon them to tell or declare where goodes stollen or lost shall become . . .*

Many Shadowhunters attempted to calm their local mundanes and direct their attention to less violent concerns; however, historical accuracy demands that we admit that many Shadowhunters took upon themselves the people's fervor for witch-burning and helped them pursue it. Some Shadowhunters thought that this new enthusiasm for stamping out demons could be directed usefully, that mundanes might become aware of and able to deal with demons on their own. Instead the Enlightenment happened, mundanes developed modern science and began to build modern technology, and belief in witchcraft became something an educated mundane would consider a silly superstition. By the end of the 1700s, across all of Europe witch-hunting had died out, and maintenance of Downworld had reverted fully to the Nephilim.

In those two-hundred-odd years, however, Downworld suffered badly from these Hunts. Warlocks, especially those with

---

*Gibson, Marion, *Witchcraft and Society in England and America*, 1550–1750 (London: Continuum International Publishing Group, 1976), 1–9.

I did not know about this. It is pretty bad, yeah.

It's not like your country or your religion behaved way better.

marks that could not be easily disguised or hidden, were especially in danger. Such "disfigurements" were seen as clear evidence of witchcraft among mundanes. Luckily, most warlocks were living among mundanes already and were used to either hiding or explaining away their warlock mark, and most were able to avoid accusation.   *I know about this, we read* The Crucible *in English class.*

In fact the Downworlders who suffered most directly from the Hunts were the werewolves. Recall that the mundanes' zeal for witch-hunting was based on a belief that witchcraft represented dalliance with "satanic forces." Just as the towns and cities were cleared of their witches, the forests of Central Europe had their werewolf populations decimated by mobs that swept through them, often with bands of hunting dogs, seeking to kill the "half-men who dally with the devil in the guise of a terrible wolf." Unlike "witches," who were regular people who had committed terrible crimes, werewolves were considered less than human and thus did not merit a trial before the death sentence was passed. Shamefully, the Council in 1612 declared its support for werewolf-hunting, arguing that those werewolves who lived in the forests rather than towns had become out of control, like wild animals, and could be put down like animals. The forests, the Clave said, contained only "savage werewolves" rather than "those respectable lycanthropes who are in control of their unusual Trait and integrated into the mundane town and city." The Council, however, knew well that the forests being hunted were full of werewolf collectives who had gone to live under a more lupine social order in places where they would not be persecuted for it; these very human werewolves were given up by the Clave and were allowed to be destroyed. Werewolves died by the hundreds, possibly the thousands.

While warlocks suffered less from the mob violence that decimated European werewolves, a different kind of damage was

Not sure I even want to ask Luke about this.

245

done to them by this anti-"satanic" fervor. Prior to this time, warlocks and Nephilim had been mostly allied, and often were close collaborators in pursuing demonic activity. We Shadowhunters possessed the tools most effective in killing demons, while the warlocks had access to magic and magical research that were of great help to us but that we could not perform ourselves (most obviously, demon-summoning). Jonathan Shadowhunter's friendship with the warlock Elphas the Unsteady set a precedent that lasted more than four hundred years.

In the wake of the witch hunts, however, a great Schism came to pass between Nephilim and warlocks. Many Shadowhunters, caught up in the fervor of the Hunts, declared warlocks to be "by nature Demonick" and fully evil. In 1640 the Clave forbade the hiring of warlocks to assist in Shadowhunter business. In some parts of the world warlocks were rounded up, or were required to make evident at all times their warlock mark (thus instantly making criminals of all those warlocks whose marks were usually hidden by clothes and the like). In other parts of the world, warlocks went into hiding, sometimes banding together for safety but more often making their way alone. These actions by the Clave worked against the interests of Shadowhunters, making it significantly more difficult for them to hunt demons. They also antagonized and dehumanized those other members of Downworld most likely to be willing partners of the Shadowhunters.

In 1688 Consul Thomas Tefereel brought about his set of well-known Reforms, which officially declared that being a werewolf and living outside mundane habitations was not in itself a capital crime. The Reforms also required Nephilim to "be careful and clear" in judging werewolves and warlocks, such that these Downworlders would be persecuted only if they were actually breaking the Law. It was not, however, until the notorious trial in 1721 of Harold and Robert Grunwald—Shadowhunter brothers who had set fire to a local tavern house in which had been gathered the entire local werewolf clan—that the werewolf hunts died away for good. The Clave was horrified by the Grunwalds' actions and, unusually, turned over the brothers to mundane authorities, who hanged them. The proactive persecution of warlocks continued in pockets around the world and dwindled only in the early nineteenth century. Warlock persecution was officially made illegal, and the laws against Shadowhunter-warlock collaboration revoked, in the First Accords in 1872. *Okay, went and asked Luke anyway. He didn't have much to say:*

• Yes, the Hunts were bad. • No, the Clave hasn't ever really made up for it, except for making it illegal now. • There are still Shadowhunters

THE ACCORDS

who think it should be illegal to "collaborate" with warlocks.

THE FIRST ACCORDS, 1872

• Easy for the Clave to take blame for something that ended three hundred years ago, think they're so great

A group of serious-looking men and a few women stand around a table rough with years, and examine the twenty-eighth draft of what, since the twenty-first draft, has become known as the Accords. This is Consul Josiah Wayland's high Victorian Council Hall; he runs things with the discipline and rigidity of a German schoolmaster. Across the table from the Council members are the various Downworlder representatives. They feel the rights of Downworlders in Reparations trials are not sufficiently spelled out.

You get the idea I think

WAYLAND, YOU FIEND!

Wayland suspects them of trying to build loopholes into the Law.

It is the hottest summer in fifty years in Alicante. Temperatures remain above ninety degrees for weeks at a time; moist hot air drapes itself over the Accords deliberations like a robe, shortening everyone's patience and goodwill. Tempers flare. A constant argument occurs about whether the windows should remain open or closed. When open they allow at least the slight relief of a cross breeze, but they also let in a population of black flies that must

248

be waved off with flyswatters. Everyone is constantly physically uncomfortable, except for the faerie and vampire representatives, who take the experience in stride, thus irritating the rest of the assembly all the more.

That Wayland would preside over what is almost certainly the most important event in modern Shadowhunter history is an interesting accident of timing. Wayland was not much loved as a Consul, and has not been remembered fondly for either his personality or his wisdom. In truth the groundwork for the Accords had been laid across the entire nineteenth century, beginning with the historic European Downworlder Treaty that was signed at the end of the Napoleonic Wars in 1815 and marked the first time an official document promised any protection under the Law for Downworlders. Most of the credit for the ideas that led to the Accords should be given to the Consul at that treaty of 1815, Shimizu-Tokugawa Katsugoro. It is a testament to Shimizu-Tokugawa's ideas and drive that even after his death in 1858, the work that led to the Accords continued until they were finally signed in 1872.

The other great hero of these First Accords was the head of the London Institute at the time, Granville Fairchild, who acted as a great peacekeeper throughout the long hot summer and constantly smoothed over relationships between the delegations at times when their clashing interests led to offense and resentment. He possessed a preternatural ability both to make the Council understand and appreciate the wishes of the Downworlder delegation, and to help the Downworlders understand and appreciate the wishes of the Nephilim. Sadly, Fairchild did not live to ratify the Accords he himself had worked so hard to complete. As negotiations were concluding, he traveled to the island of Cyprus to offer his expertise in demonology to the Institute there. The Cypriot Nephilim were fighting the Greater Demon

Stheno, who was ravaging the countryside. There Fairchild died, as befits a Shadowhunter, in battle with Stheno. Though they were drastically different men, Fairchild and Consul Wayland had a great friendship, and Wayland dedicated the signing of the Accords to Fairchild's memory.

(In an unusual end to the story, Stheno was eventually dispatched back to the Void in Scotland in 1894 by a team of English Shadowhunters; though Stheno was in disguise, he was recognized because he was wearing Granville Fairchild's favorite Ukrainian fur hat, which had been a gift from Wayland.) *Ha!*

These First Accords were opposed heavily by some Shadowhunters, mostly those who stood to lose significant income as a result of the proposed Reforms. (See "Spoils," page 178.) Luckily, compromises were found that allowed the Accords to be ratified and signed. The final draft, the thirty-third, was agreed upon near the end of the summer of 1872. Fifty signers were present to ratify it: ten vampires, ten werewolves, ten warlocks, ten faeries, and ten Nephilim. Vampire representative Aron Benedek famously described the final document as a "compromise of compromises," but in truth the skeleton of the subsequent Accords was fully in place with this first agreement. The Accords that have followed have hewn to its model more often than not.

Among the landmark resolutions adopted as part of these First Accords were:

- The declaration of Downworlders as beings with souls, and thus entitled to the protections due to humans.
- The revoking of Laws making it illegal for Downworlders to adopt mundane children.
- The granting to Downworlders of the right to a court trial when accused of breaking the Law; no longer could Shadowhunters adjudge them guilty of crimes and punish them immediately.

- Legal language restricting the penalties that could be
placed on Downworlders, to prevent punishment out of
proportion to the crime.
- The granting of Downworlders' right to their own
internal organizational schemes—vampire clans, wolf
packs, faerie courts, et cetera—without interference
from the Clave. In fact, the Accords made membership
in one of these internal organizations a requirement for
Downworlders; "unaffiliated" vampires or werewolves
were considered rogue and were not afforded the same
protections under the Law.
- Acknowledgment of the Nephilim as the official
law-keeping force of Downworld, and agreement
by the Downworlders to abide by Covenant Law.
Acknowledgment of the theoretical body of Heaven,
through its representative Raziel, as the ultimate
authority over our world.

It is interesting to examine the updates in the Accords over
the years, and how the Accords today differ from the original
document signed those many years ago. The major differences
include:

- Increasingly detailed and specific language about the
rights of Downworlders in criminal trials. The need for
more and more legalism in the Accords came about
as Consuls and Inquisitors varied wildly in how they
interpreted things, sometimes adopting draconian rules
against Downworlder groups, who had little recourse
but to try to get the rules made more specific in the next
Accords. Interestingly, the criminal law section of the
Accords is now treated as a separate document and is
framed by a different group of representatives—ones
with legal expertise—from those who write the rest of the

Accords. This is in part because the criminal law section of the Accords is now significantly longer than the entire rest of the Accords put together. This separate document is, however, the only place where a Downworlder's right to trial is officially recognized by the Nephilim, and so the document has grown in importance with each successive Accords.

· A much stronger declaration of the rights of mundanes to live their lives unimpeded by the vicissitudes of Downworlders. It was at the Seventh Accords, for instance, that it first became illegal for vampires to keep subjugates.

· During the time of the first three Accords, warlocks were habitually summoning demons at the request of Nephilim. Technically this was illegal. The Fourth Accords specifically made it legal for warlocks to do whatever magic was deemed necessary in the course of a Nephilim investigation.

These and other such social reforms teach us that the spirit of the Accords is alive in Idris, and that we continue to refine and ever improve relations between Idris and Downworld.

So progressive, we couldn't murder Downworlders in the street anymore.

Big change, though—from "Downworlders are basically demons" to "Downworlders are basically humans."

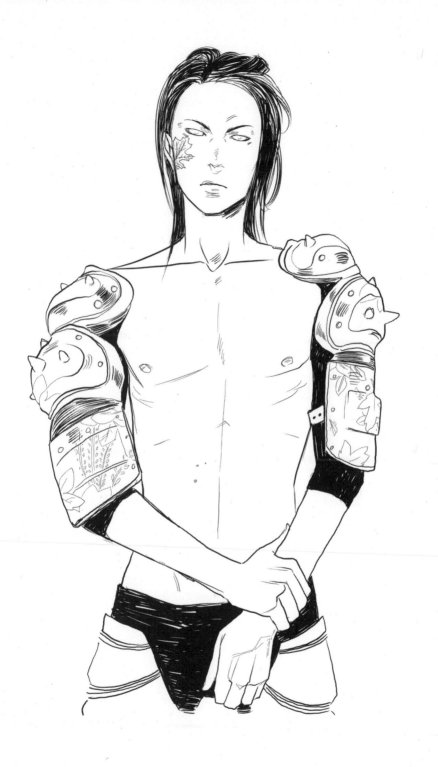

APPENDIX B

THE NINTH ACCORDS, 1992

Addendum to the *Shadowhunter's Codex*, 27th edition, added 2002
By Christopher Makepeace, Institute Head, Melbourne, Australia

*I hereby render unconditional obedience to the Circle
and its principles. . . . I will be ready to risk my life at
any time for the Circle, in order to preserve the purity
of the bloodlines of Idris, and for the mortal world with
whose safety we are charged.*

—Loyalty oath of the Circle

The Accords have never had the unanimous support of the Clave. Almost every Accords negotiation has drawn protests, objections, internal squabbles from among the Nephilim. Those in far-flung territories, especially, with sparser populations, have often argued that Downworlder relations in such "wilds" require a looser hand, that the restrictions on Shadowhunter behavior in the Accords severely limit their ability to do their jobs.

These arguments have been heated and impassioned. Tempers have flared. Respected members of the Clave have stormed out of the Accords Hall in fury. Certain Downworlders and certain Shadowhunters have had to be carefully seated far from one another in the negotiation chambers.

At heart, though, the Nephilim's and the Downworlders' aims have aligned. We have all wanted peace. Everyone has, at root, wanted peace. Until the Circle.

Valentine Morgenstern, the only living son of a widely respected and long-standing Nephilim family, and his followers, disrupted the Accords. Not disrupted—invaded. I was there. Some have, in the years following, downplayed the horror and the violence of that day, to paint Morgenstern and his followers as noble dissidents, protestors using dramatic actions to make their point. But I was there.

Let us not mince words. The Circle despised Downworlders. They believed in the purity of humans and the impurity of Downworld, believed that Downworlders were at their root demons, and believed that Downworlders should be slaughtered to keep the world pure for humans. They viewed those Shadowhunters who disagreed with them as complicit in the profanity they believed Downworlders brought to our world. The Circle members were not protestors; they were violent fanatics.

(It is worth noting, in fairness to certain families, that many of the original members of the Circle, and many of the closest of Morgenstern's original followers, had before the Accords fled from him because of the extremity of his views and the brutality of his plan, and were not present for the events in the Accords Hall. Not all of Valentine's followers went along forever with his heinous crimes.)

Like so many other Shadowhunters, the Circle were in the Accords Hall that day, among the vast audience of Nephilim and Downworlders in the gallery awaiting the signing of these Ninth Accords. Unbeknownst to anyone else present, they had smuggled demonic weapons into the Hall—their fanaticism was such that they would use the tools of the explicitly demonic if they believed it would satisfy their supposedly noble ends. At the moment when the Accords were presented for signing, the Circle, as one body, rose and bared their weapons. Panic broke instantly over the Hall like a wave in a storm.

Amid the tumult it became clear that a number of Downworlder groups had been aware of the Circle's plans and had laid in wait outside the Hall in secret to fight them. At the explosion of chaos these groups burst into the Hall and joined the battle. In truth this was not the shock it might have been. Valentine had been vocal in his protests for many months, and many expected some demonstration from him and his followers during the Accords—but nothing like the melee that occurred.

To attempt to describe the disarray and carnage of battle calls to my mind age-old clichés that cannot convey the power of the moment: *It was horrible. It will stay with me forever. It was worse than your imagining.* But all of these things are true. Good men and women were cut down in front of me, for no better reason than that the blood spattering their Accords robes would highlight the message of the Circle's attack. Downworlders whose only crime was a demonic parent, or a demonic disease beyond their control, were murdered for having the misfortune of being present. Council members and Downworlder representatives alike shouted themselves hoarse, trying to restore order, unable to be heard over the din of metal smashing against metal and into human bodies.

I can close my eyes today, ten years later, as I write these words in my quiet office atop the tall crystal towers of the Melbourne Institute, and the smell of blood and the sound of slaughter come back to me as if I were still there. I think that probably the memory will never depart the dark places behind my eyes.

Worst harmed in the battle were the Shadowhunters unaffiliated with the Circle. They were killed, often indiscriminately, both purposefully by the Circle and accidentally by Downworlders who believed them to be among the enemy. Nevertheless, with the help of the Downworlder armies, the Circle was beaten back, and fled. They were only barely defeated. Valentine Morgenstern fled the Hall and retreated to his own house on the outskirts of Alicante, where he set a great fire and burned himself to death, along with his wife and his young child. Defeated, Valentine must have known that his life was forfeit; he was guilty of the greatest of Nephilim crimes, the murder of Nephilim. It is only fitting that he dispatched two last innocent victims, his own family, as his final act in the world.

259

ACE of CUPS.

· · ·

The Uprising ended in failure. The Nephilim and the Downworlders treated their wounded and saw to their dead. A great funeral was held in Angel Square in Alicante to honor the memory of those lost. Many surviving members of the Circle threw themselves upon the mercy of the Clave, and cooperated with the investigations into the whereabouts of those still loyal to Valentine. There was much speculation that the Accords had fallen apart, that peace between Idris and Downworld was impossible.

But the Ninth Accords were signed. In a stroke of irony Valentine's terrible acts helped to uphold the Shadow World's commitment to the Accords' passage. It had been a difficult negotiation that year, full of clashing personalities and strong opinions, but after the Uprising a great sense of fraternity was felt by Downworlder and Shadowhunter representatives alike, united against their common foe, and they were able to ratify the Accords only a few weeks later.

The Tenth Accords (2007), just terrible for everyone.

THINGS TURNED OUT OKAY, THOUGH, RIGHT? GUYS?

The Great and Tragic Love of Jonathan Shadowhunter and David the Silent, by ~~Clary Fray, Aged 17~~

SIMON IT WAS BY SIMON NOT ME

JONATHAN SHADOWHUNTER: I am Jonathan Shadowhunter, and I am about to form a holy order of warriors to defend Earth from demons! I am louche and aristocratic and callow!

DAVID: I am David and I witnessed something truly horrific in a cave and as a result I have taken a vow of silence and sworn myself to killing demons. I am only thinking these things, rather than saying them out loud, because I have taken a vow of silence.

JONATHAN: I throw myself at demons indiscriminately!

DAVID: Verily, you shall be killed if you keep doing that. You need an influence of calm and meditative spirit in this mission. It is not just a war; it is a holy war. Meditate with me.

JONATHAN: This meditating business is very nice, and I feel more balanced and together than ever before, but have you noticed that we are supposed to be demon hunters but in fact neither of us has actually killed a demon in many moons?

DAVID: Are you suggesting that only the combination of both your rash bravery and my levelheaded thinkiness can hope to defeat the darkness, rather than either alone?

JONATHAN: . . . No, but that's much better than what I was suggesting, so let's go with that!

DAVID: We kill demons awesomely now! We go on adventures and repeatedly save each other's lives!

JONATHAN: Oh, David, I would trust you with my life!

DAVID: Oh, Jonathan, I would sacrifice my own life for your holy mission! [He almost does.] I regret nothing.

JONATHAN: (weeping) David, you must return to me! I need you! I cannot do this thing without you!

DAVID: Lo, I return!

~~**JONATHAN:** Zounds! I feel a great stirring in my pantaloons.~~

~~**DAVID:** What doth the pantalo~~

SIMON I WILL KILL YOU

DISCUSSION QUESTIONS AND THINGS TO TRY

1. With which of the founders of the Nephilim—Jonathan, David, or Abigail—do you feel a bond? Why? What about their lives can inform the way you live your own?

Um, I guess Abigail because she's the only girl, Codex. I mean, really? At least boys get two different people to choose from. Abigail's defining feature is she's female.

Some would say Abigail's defining feature was that she learned how to work the very material of Heaven on a forge, and then she built a gigantic fortress and never came out again. I don't see that as a reason not to feel a bond with her.

Where do you want to get lunch?

MY PSYCHIC VAMPIRE POWERS SAY YOU WANT NOODLES.

I always want noodles.

YOUR PSYCHIC NOODLE POWERS DEPEND ON THEM. True.

What are you guys, twelve? Stop passing the thing back and forth.

HISTORY OF THE CODEX

Did You Know? *How could you possibly care?* The first edition of *The Shadowhunter's Codex* is a hand-illuminated book written in Vulgar Latin, on pages of vellum. It can be seen in a carefully preserved display among the treasures of Alicante. For many years this first edition was believed to have been written by Jonathan Shadowhunter, in his own hand, and thus was dated to the late eleventh century. Modern research and dating techniques have, unfortunately, revealed that this date is not correct, and the first edition instead dates to the early thirteenth century, almost a hundred years after Jonathan Shadowhunter's believed date of death. Its author and its illuminator, whether the same person or different, remain unknown. Many different Enclaves of Shadowhunters in Europe have laid claim to being the rightful inheritors of the original *Codex*, but no evidence has ever arisen to allow a definitive claim. In any event it is logical to understand the *Codex* as a document dating from after the deaths of the first Shadowhunters, when the Nephilim of Idris were actively working to find recruits to their mission and to drastically expand their numbers and their geographical reach. The *Codex* would have provided an expeditious method of teaching the literate, at the very least, about the Shadow World and its denizens.

The first edition of the *Codex* produced on a printing press is not nearly as mysterious. The *Codex* was first printed, in German, on the presses of the Institute at Frankfurt-am-Main in what was then the Holy Roman Empire. It was brought to that Institute from Heidelberg, where a group of Nephilim had been studying demonology in collaboration with scholars of the university there. It is unknown how many copies were made, but of them, forty-eight survive. Of these, several can be found in Alicante, and at least one can be found at each Great Library. The rest are spread among smaller Institutes, mostly in Central Europe, and a small number of Shadowhunter private collections.

This edition of the *Codex* is a minor revision of the twenty-seventh edition, first published in 1990. Only material related to the Ninth Accords has been added. *I CARE.*

Don't you quote Star Wars at me, Lewis.

NOTES:
DO NOT DOODLE IN THIS SPACE

NOTES AREA

Please use this blank space provided to practice Marks. Note:
Please practice your Marks with a waster and not with a real stele.
Paper is too fragile to withstand the force of heavenly fire.

ARTIST ACKNOWLEDGMENTS

Rebecca Guay provided us with the frontispiece, a study of the primary players from the Mortal Instruments books.

Charles Vess supplied the endpiece, a similar study of the characters of the Infernal Devices. (That's the London Institute they're frolicking upon.)

Michael Wm. Kaluta produced the chapter headings, and understood what we meant when we said, "Do it like an old-school gaming manual."

John Dollar illustrated the history of the Nephilim, choosing what to illustrate from the text himself, rather than being given a specific list of requested subjects.

Theo Black was commissioned to do two pieces of faerie-themed art and then sent us five. We used all five.

Elisabeth Alba's quickly dashed-off practice sketches were good enough to print, but we were glad we waited for the actual finished pieces. She contributed beautiful, mostly pencil-based work across the whole Codex.

Jim Nelson also contributed beautiful work across the whole Codex, but most important, he added three new demons to the Shadowhunter universe. They are wonderfully disgusting and we are proud to have them.

Cassandra Jean as Clary Fray. Cassandra Jean drew all over this thing, and filled the back of it with portraits.

Michael McCartney at Simon & Schuster designed the book, placed the art, and was very, very patient with our many detail-oriented requests.

And of course, thanks to **Valerie Freire** for her rune designs and her inspiration.